Advance Praise for *Business is Business*

"America is built on families and entrepreneurs. In *Business is Business*, Kathy Kolbe and Amy Bruske have given us a primer on how to build on these two pillars and create thriving family businesses that can flex and grow with each new generation. If you are running a family business, or thinking of taking the leap, then this book will be your essential guide."

—MARCUS BUCKINGHAM, internationally renowned thought leader
and business expert, NYT best-selling author of
First, Break All the Rules and *Stand Out 2.0*

"All family-owned businesses are going to have ups and downs—but with Kathy Kolbe and Amy Bruske as your guides, your potential for success is greater than ever. Read *Business is Business*, and you'll see what I mean."

—KEN BLANCHARD, coauthor of *The New One Minute Manager* and
Collaboration Begins with You

"Combining frameworks they originally developed with over 20 years of joint experience running and working with family owned businesses, Kathy Kolbe and Amy Bruske present a wealth of great ideas and examples of how to run this type of business. *Business is Business* presents concepts based on the Conative Theory of human behavior, uses them to explain ineffective behavior in family-owned businesses, and then goes on to apply these same concepts to suggest practical ways to overcome organizational dysfunctions. Although Kolbe and Bruske focus on family-owned businesses, their approach is applicable to all businesses. This is a special book!"

—JERRY I PORRAS, professor emeritus at Stanford Business School and
coauthor of *Built to Last: Successful Habits of Visionary Companies*

"The very qualities that give family businesses monumental competitive advantages are often the same qualities that suffocate innovation and accelerate demise. Decoding this paradox has not only been the lifework of Kathy Kolbe and Amy Bruske; it's now the written work of their life. Brilliantly conceived, beautifully written."

—TOM DEANS, PhD, author of *Every Family's Business* and *Willing Wisdom*

"In *Business is Business*, Kolbe and Bruske tackle the most challenging people problems all family-business owners face. This powerful must-read book outlines proven solutions for leveraging family members' strengths, dealing with communication challenges, and developing future leaders."

—DAN SULLIVAN, founder of The Strategic Coach, Inc.

"Our family business has grown more than 20 percent annually since we began using the Kolbe methods described in this book. It has been essential in understanding how to work with my wife, Maria, and many other family members who all have an emotional attachment to the business and has helped us create ideal roles as we prosper together."

—ANTONIO DOS SANTOS, CEO of Medisca Corp

"Before we had the tips now available in this book, my husband, father, and I experienced a great deal of pain hiring—and having to fire—other family members in our midsized family business. We also suffered from miscommunications among ourselves. That awful strain didn't stop until we started to follow Kolbe's advice. It also dramatically improved communication among ourselves and with our clients. It enabled us to thrive while working together."

—DENISE (DENNY) GUSTIN-PIAZZA, president of WealthPlanners, LLC

"Kolbe has had a monstrous impact on my life, on my family's and all of my businesses, which have involved over 40 family members. It not only helped us grow our business; it helped us understand how each family member naturally operates. After we started using the Kolbe process as a family, we used it to build the teams around us. The result was that we quadrupled our revenue over a five-year period."

—JERRY LUJAN, owner of Manuel Lujan Insurance Agencies

"I've worked with family-owned businesses for over 30 years and find this is the single best book for overcoming the unique challenges of working with family companies. The wisdom in this book is enormous, yet it is presented in simple, organized, and innovative formats. *Business is Business* will help you—with practical Reality Checks—to solve many of the puzzles that have sunk otherwise viable companies."

—RAMON G. CORRALES, PhD, CEO of Integral Mastery Center

"The Reality Checks in this book have greatly improved my understanding of myself and how to build our business. I am especially thankful that they led to the mending of a near-broken bond between me and my son. Using them opened communication that had never been there, either in my managing or parenting. There's tremendous value in the previously missing explanations to the differing ways even family members need to solve problems. I wish everyone was aware of this very clear advice on how to make it work to work together."

—DON MUNCE, founder and chairman of the board of the
National Research Center for College & University Admissions

"This book is filled with substantive information that can enhance your understanding of human behavior and increase your productivity—both at work and in life."

—NIDO R. QUBEIN, president of High Point University and founder of the
National Speakers Association Foundation

"This book will save much of the heartache and aggravation I've seen in over 30 years of consulting with family businesses and, more importantly, with the people who own them. Not only is it a powerful resource for those family businesses, but it will help almost any business!"

—TONY ROSE, senior partner and CPA at Rose, Snyder, & Jacobs, LLP, and
author of *Five Eyes on the Fence* and *Say Hello to the Elephants*

"Every good business is a family business, whether literally or figuratively. The key to making it work is putting truth at the center of everything, particularly when building and running teams. This book is an essential read for anyone building for the long haul with people they love."

—JOSH JONES-DILWORTH, founder and CEO of JDI Consulting

"As an author, speaker, and consultant, I needed to learn how to work more effectively with my team. Unfortunately, my lack of understanding caused unnecessary strain with my most important relationship—with my wife, Diane. Kolbe Wisdom™ helped us structure our roles and responsibilities in a way that dramatically improved our performance and the quality of life we now enjoy."

—JOE CALHOON, business growth strategist, author, and speaker

"The power of knowing your striving instincts creates an incredible advantage in a family run business. I have utilized the principles and strategies in this book in working with my husband for over two decades. The need to address tough decisions and 'keep the love alive' as a couple is a difficult dance. Kolbe has helped us navigate through these often treacherous waters."

—MARI D. MARTIN, president of Performance Strategies Group, Inc.

Also by Kathy Kolbe

The Conative Connection

Pure Instinct

Powered by Instinct

Striving Zones

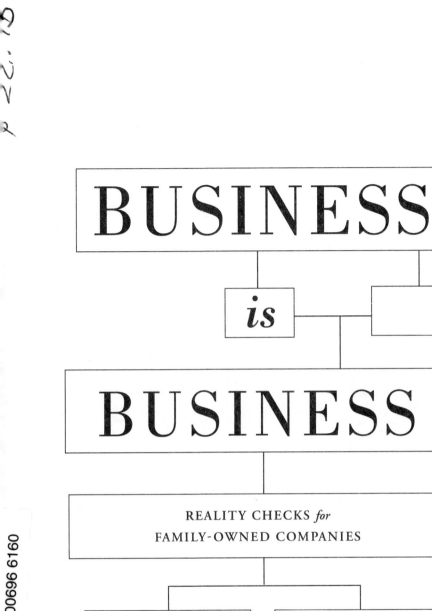

BUSINESS

is

BUSINESS

REALITY CHECKS *for*
FAMILY-OWNED COMPANIES

KATHY KOLBE   AMY BRUSKE

GREENLEAF
BOOK GROUP PRESS

This publication is designed to provide accurate and authoritative information in regard to the subject matter covered. It is sold with the understanding that the publisher and author are not engaged in rendering legal, accounting, or other professional services. If legal advice or other expert assistance is required, the services of a competent professional should be sought.

Published by Greenleaf Book Group Press
Austin, Texas
www.gbgpress.com

Distributed by Greenleaf Book Group

For ordering information or special discounts for bulk purchases, please contact Greenleaf Book Group at PO Box 91869, Austin, TX 78709, 512.891.6100.

Design and composition by Greenleaf Book Group
Cover design by Greenleaf Book Group
Cover image: ©istockphoto.com/DianeLabombarbe

The following terms are trademarks owned by Kathy Kolbe or Kolbe Corp:
Action Modes®, Apt™ Careers, Commitment Clarifier®, Comparisons: A to A™, Comparisons: A to B™, Comparisons: A to C™, Conables®, Dynamynd®, Kolbe RightFit™, Kolbe A™ Index, Kolbe B™ Index, Kolbe C™ Index, Kolbe R™ Index, Kolbe Y™ Index, Kolbe Certification™, Kolbe Creative Process™, Kolbe Strengths™, Kolbe TeamSuccess®, Kolbe Wisdom™, Leadership Analytics™, Natural Advantage™, Takes Two™, and Think-ercise!®

Cataloging-in-Publication data is available.

Print ISBN: 978-1-62634-373-3

eBook ISBN: 978-1-62634-374-0

Part of the Tree Neutral® program, which offsets the number of trees consumed in the production and printing of this book by taking proactive steps, such as planting trees in direct proportion to the number of trees used: www.treeneutral.com

TreeNeutral®

Printed in the United States of America on acid-free paper

16 17 18 19 20 21   10 9 8 7 6 5 4 3 2 1

First Edition

We dedicate this book to an amazing group of family business clients, many of whose stories we share here. They have become friends, cohorts, and coconspirators of creativity. We've learned from them, laughed with them, and cried with them. Their openly sharing their deepest pains and hard-earned gains inspired us to write this book.

Contents

About the Authors xi

Introduction 1

Chapter 1: Creating Sustainable Success 7

Chapter 2: Protecting Values: Keeping Tabs on
the Truth 21

Chapter 3: How Hard Should You Work? 35

Chapter 4: Banking on Trust. 53

Chapter 5: Boundaries That Build Better FOBs 73

Chapter 6: Telling It Like It Is—Or Not 91

Chapter 7: Developing Living Assets. 109

Chapter 8: Inciting Next-Gen Ambition 139

Chapter 9: Knowing When Teams Won't Work. 155

Chapter 10: Orchestrating Transitions 173

Chapter 11: Graceful Exits 193

Acknowledgments 205

Appendix 207

Glossary. 225

Selected Kolbe Products and Services for
Family Businesses 231

Index 237

About the Authors

Kathy Kolbe and Amy Bruske have succeeded by trusting their instincts.

Google "Kathy Kolbe" and you'll find out she's *the* global leader in discovering and accessing the power of human instincts. She's done the brain research to prove the relevance of her Kolbe Theory of Conation to individual and organizational success.

Kathy resurrected the word "conation," which spell-check changes to cognition. Conation was defined by the early Greek philosophers Plato and Aristotle as the aspect of the mind that deals with actions, reactions, and interactions. She traced conation's history through centuries of misguided attempts to tie it to emotions, right up to the abandonment of it by Swiss psychiatrist/psychotherapist Jung as "too difficult to disengage" from both the cognitive and the affective part of the mind.

Kathy was the first person to connect conative behavior to instinctive drives, which she postulated as the source of the patterns of mental energy commonly known as *modus operandi*, or a person's MO.

After years of studying the connection between instincts and behaviors, Kathy was writing the book *The Conative Connection* when she was almost killed in a car accident. While she was coping with the resulting traumatic brain injury, she met Amy, the daughter of a very kind man who was helping Kathy heal. Amy and her father were also healing after the death of his wife, her mother.

Both Kathy and Amy were fighting to stay conative during a period of cognitive and emotional turmoil. That meant they had to keep working at fulfilling their life purposes. Amy went on to college; Kathy went to physical rehab. After more than a year of not being able to read and write, Kathy returned to a book she had been writing about conation—and began to reinvigorate a business she came close to losing. (All but three of her 27 employees had left, believing she would never be able to come back to it.)

A year later Amy's father, Will Rapp, and Kathy called Amy at college to say they were trusting their instincts. Despite knowing each other for only a short time, they were going to marry. Amy's response was to hang up. She immediately called back with the basic message: "*Whatever.*"

How, against all odds, has this unlikely pairing of mother and step-daughter resulted in a highly successful business partnership, a close personal relationship, and an ability to write this book together? Their desire to help others achieve the same goals has prompted them to share the *Dos* and *Don't*s and Reality Checks provided in these pages.

Footnote

Will and Kathy's son, David, has also been in the business for over 20 years. The three other adult children in Kathy and Will's blended family are equally admired professionals.

Both Amy and Kathy are award-winning consultants/advisors to business owners, C-level leaders, and mid-level managers in family-owned businesses (FOBs), as well as to Fortune 500 companies. Both are also sought-after speakers. With more than 3,000 FOBs as clients, they have observed and discussed more problems and solutions than could be described in a book ten times this size.

As mother and daughter (they do not use the term "stepdaughter"), working together for more than two decades, Kathy and Amy have personally experienced every situation brought up in this book. Neither recalls a time when she wished she were working anywhere else.

Introduction

When we copresent, or work together on a client engagement, there is usually no reason to mention that we are related. We're professionals sharing our expertise. Yet, we've discovered that it's important when working with family-owned businesses (FOBs) to explain our family connection.

> *"What! You're family? You've made it work? Really? How?"*

The fact that we've been there, done that, makes the advice more meaningful.

> *"Okay, so you're not just giving us the theory of family business management," clients say. "You're telling it like it is. You're giving us the unvarnished truth."*

You bet we are. We're not afraid to tell it like it is.
Our goal is to help your business shine, which, we realize, never happens without hard work and filling the cracks as you go.

Do the benefits outweigh the burdens of working in a family business?

Yes—if you do it right.

Key advantages of being in an FOB include

- Having the freedom to act on your instincts.

- Having the peace of mind that comes from working with people you trust.

- Finding joy in common efforts and shared accomplishments.

What about the burdens?

An FOB becomes a burden if you violate two major issues we will discuss throughout this book. They are

- Glossing over problems, hoping they won't damage family relationships.

- Taking work problems home with you, creating a mere façade of quality personal time.

Working with family adds a layer of complexity to the already daunting task of owning and operating a business. It's horrific when family members (FMs) discover breaches of trust or when they don't share workplace values. Therefore, we had to put those issues in the first chapters.

There are times when relatives in a business realize that they have to double down on their efforts to keep the company solvent. Walking away is not an option.

Many founders have questioned why they ever started the business:

> "What was I thinking?" Rita asked. "I could have worked
> for a corporation that would have given me more security,
> a heck of a lot more time off—and I wouldn't have had any

guilt about how it's all working out for the family members I brought in."

"We're doing fine financially," said spouses who are business partners, "but working together is destroying our personal life. It seems we have to choose our company or our marriage."

"It's too much drama for too little dough!" said Herb. "I'm tired of the complaints from all the relatives who don't think my decisions are fair. They seemed to think they were getting cushy jobs where they wouldn't have to put in much effort."

Solutions are not always easy. But there are patterns to the problems.

Understanding what often goes wrong has helped us come up with ways to avoid the traps that families who work together fall into all too often. Now we know and can share with others what has and hasn't worked. We can pass on information that we wish *we* had learned from someone else. Not that we think you can avoid all the pitfalls or that you don't need to learn from your own mistakes.

We believe understanding what's behind our guidelines will help you and your family. We can give you tips—something as simple as telling you to drop the family nouns (Mom, Dad, Son, Daughter, Sis) at work—to help you jump over a hurdle you may not have even seen.

We've been blindsided more than once because we didn't have these guidelines as a reference. Very few rules were passed down to us. We were pretty fearless in taking on the challenges we knew were ahead of us, but we've both had to learn by confronting the ones we didn't foresee. As we've dealt with problems with client after client, we've been able to distinguish between what is generally applicable to most FOBs and what might be unique to a particular family.

When we share stories about others, we've changed the demographics, names, and businesses, so don't bother guessing whether any of these are family businesses you know. It's gratifying to have more positive outcomes than we can share in this book. Unfortunately, too many families have not known the kind of help that's available.

Seven principles for success of a family business

Defining success for a family business is complicated. We selected factors that impact sustainability of the business and quality of life for family members and non–family members (NFMs) who work within it.

To us, a successful FOB

- Honors and maintains the family values.

- Addresses the fears and concerns of FMs and NFMs.

- Manages finances so profits can be distributed for current and future family needs and benefits.

- Deals with the dual relationships that exist between NFMs and FMs in both family and workplace contexts.

- Addresses both personal and business issues with FMs outside the business.

- Establishes proper boundaries so that decisions are ethical, practical, and therefore, easy to make and to explain.

- Gives all FMs and NFMs the freedom to be themselves.

We're not going to tell you how to get rich, or how to deal with the strict father or the controlling mother or any other psychological issues within family structures. We are not financial advisors or psychologists. Our expertise is organization development and human productivity.

Our goal is to help you find joy while developing a stable and sustainable business.

This book focuses on how you can make wise choices about when Business is Business—and Family is Family. The advice in it has proven to be important for the business growth and personal development in profitable family enterprises. As we continue to grow our own businesses, we both find value in going through the same Reality Checks we put at the end of each chapter. We have not learned all we need to know. We hope that what we do know, however, will assist others who strive in family businesses.

CHAPTER 1

Creating Sustainable Success

Most family-owned businesses (FOBs) start as an individual effort (aka solopreneur), or a partnership between a couple of people who are related to one another. Rarely does someone actually intend to manage the people they love. Rational people realize that the theme song for FOBs (much like Taylor Swift's breakup message in many of her songs) could be *I love you very much, but I don't like what you are doing.*

Kathy, who grew up in a family business, vowed never to work in it as an adult. Why, then, did she found a family business?

She didn't. She started a business on her own in order to fulfill a mission. Her company, now known as Kolbe Corp, didn't become an FOB for over a decade. For the many years while she was single-parenting two kids, she was struggling on her own to build a business.

When her new, trusted spouse decided to share her mission and contribute his complementary instincts to that effort, it made all future disasters easier to digest.

By the time other family members (FMs) got involved, Kathy had discovered how to use (or not) each FM's best method for contributing to their shared purposes. Kathy and her husband, Will Rapp, also knew it wasn't just about abilities; it was about levels of commitment. With more family involved, the revolving door of training people who move on was likely to close. It was time to build an internal brain trust.

After more than 40 years, it's evident that the business Amy is now president of has proven to have sustainable success.

There'd better be a good reason to get involved

Business is Business. When FMs come into a business, they need to be able to add value to it—and the business needs to add value to their lives. If that's not the case, don't risk jeopardizing your family's economic security as well as ruining family relationships to get into an FOB. Imagine taking this risk, and then failing to grow it into a profitable, mature, and sustainable organization. When you fail in an FOB, you take the family's security with you.

Public companies are even more likely to fail than FOBs are, yet it's sad that after all the commitment and angst founders put into FOBs, fewer than 15 percent of them (according to multiple sources) make it to a third generation. A primary reason for this is often the poor selection and placement of FMs within the businesses. Leaders usually pick and choose FMs based on emotional need or wants rather than wise business selection practices. Placement is even worse. It is often sexist and ageist. Eldest sons get top jobs. Daughters rarely run departments that are driven by profit and loss statements.

We suggest that our FOB clients ask themselves the following questions when they are considering hiring an FM. Both the family members who are employees and those considering joining the business should answer these questions and discuss them. Be clear about your answers before moving forward:

- Do you have shared values?

- How would the business benefit from the personal strengths of the FM candidate, including both natural conative abilities and skills/experience?

- Would the owner/founder and other decision makers give the candidate the freedom to act on his or her strengths?

- How would the business benefit from these contributions?

- How would the FM benefit from joining the team?

Building on strengths

The basic ingredients of sustainable success we've discovered and thoroughly tested in other FOBs are these:

- **Identifying and using** the three ways everyone needs to contribute: thinking, feeling, and doing.

- **Providing roles** that give each FM the freedom to contribute their natural conative, instinct-based strengths to the business.

- **Forming collaborative teams** that work effectively to provide solutions to the business's problems and opportunities.

If an FOB doesn't have a process in place that sticks to these guidelines, this is what can happen.

> Bringing his son, Billy, into his financial services firm seemed so wise to Drew. Billy was smart and had an MBA. Now that he was married, Billy was ready to settle down into a stable career that would give him financial security. It would be

> great for Drew to be able to eventually hand the business
> to his son. It would ensure that his clients had continu-
> ity when he retires. It would be especially wonderful, they
> both thought, because they had always gotten along so
> well together, sharing hobbies and family travel.

It had seemed like a no-brainer, but it turned into a night-mare. Bringing Billy into the business ended up harming it and their relationship.

A simple Reality Check that covers all the mental factors (see the appendix) discussed in the pages that follow could have prevented this from happening. It was predictable that Billy would not be a good fit for the role Drew wanted him to fill. Here's what we've found that makes it so predictable.

The three mental factors/parts of the mind behind job success

Billy needed to know more about the financial advice he was giving before he gave it. This is a cognitive factor (aka thinking).

THINKING—WHAT YOU *KNOW*

> *Cognitive*—skills, knowledge, reason, experience,
> education, or capabilities

How smart Billy was turned out—as it usually does—to be only a small part of what he needed to do to succeed in the business. In fact, getting A's in school does not forecast success in the field of financial services.

"Brainiacs lack common sense," some people say. While that is not true, it is true that a high IQ does not ensure adequate knowledge and the professional skills to be able to help people make financial decisions that satisfy their needs and desires.

Understanding *what* makes people tick helps, and that's exactly what Drew did not understand about Billy. He did not realize that Billy had not *learned* common sense business judgment prior to coming into the family firm. Billy's years of sports-related camps and internships were of little value in the business. His lack of experience showed up when dealing with clients and staff. People liked him, but they did not respect him.

Here's another example of a cognitive, or thinking-based, issue.

> Clare has an MBA, but the sister with an undergraduate degree in journalism turned out to be the better business-woman. Her uncle had seen that in her sister from the time she had convinced him to put ads in her fledgling neighborhood magazine.
>
> "I'd say both of them are smart," the uncle said, "but Clare is not the natural deal maker; her sister was more entrepreneurial. Clare, by doing what the books taught her to do, would be better suited to working in larger corporations."

A particular type of FOB, the professional firm, requires FMs to have specific types of knowledge. These firms involve relatives who are lawyers, doctors, accountants, appraisers, realtors, and such. In many of these situations, the skills of a parent offer a shelter under which the next generation can learn the business—once they have the credentials to be in it.

"She's riding on her father's coattails," is often true in these FOBs. But one day, the daughter will be billing more hours or selling more homes, and the parent can bow out. It's a nice setup when it works. But first, it requires the learned ability to do what needs to be done.

FEELING—WHAT YOU *WANT*

> ***Affective*—Values, desires, motivation, attitudes, preferences, or emotions**

Drew is highly motivated to make every single business deal a home run. Billy was fine just getting a walk to first base. Drew thought he could coach Billy to a higher level of ambition. The affect between them changed when Drew realized his son was not as concerned about helping the team win as Drew wished he were.

Any fan watching Billy play could have predicted he would get traded. But it's usually tough for a parent to come to grips with that.

If FOB leaders dissuade their youngsters from chasing their dream careers, is it any different from Drew trying to turn Billy into the person he dreams Billy could be?

FOB owners often tell us, "They had to get it out of their system." And, "I didn't want them moping around here as if it were a slave camp." They also say, "The worst thing I ever did was try to make my kid do things my way."

DOING—HOW YOU WILL AND WON'T TAKE ACTION

> ***Conative*—Actions, ReActions, and CounterActions: Instinct-based natural drives, necessity, innate force, mental energy, or talents**

Conation is an internal, unchanging, unconscious attribute that is not altered by education, coaching, counseling, self-help manuals, parenting, or pleading. It is derived from subconscious, unalterable instincts, which come in a set of attributes or traits that are the modes of a person's natural method of striving, or modus operandi (MO). They determine how we act, react, and interact.

As every parent knows, kids come into the world being their unique selves. Their conative actions become acts of will when someone interferes with their control over their innate, instinct-driven patterns of behavior. (Watch two-year-olds to see the stubbornness of human instincts.)

Individuals have no control over the modalities of their conative behaviors, yet they do have the power to determine when they will use this resource. Learning to exercise this power appropriately is a big part of gaining maturity.

"Taking charge of your own destiny" assumes that the individual has the self-determination or free will to direct the uses of his or her conative strengths. You can offer your FMs opportunities to work in an FOB, but how they will perform there is entirely under their own control.

People are predictable in the way they will act because of the instinctive and distinctive patterns within an individual's conative makeup.

The existence of conation was identified by the ancient philosophers, but it has been ignored by academics. The Kolbe Theory has brought it to light by discovering the four universal instincts that drive our unique methods of problem solving when we are striving.

Instincts are the bedrock, hardwiring, and DNA-equivalent of the mind. Like a fingerprint or blood type, a person is born with this conative MO and can count on it to be there for a lifetime. And there is nothing you can do to change that—no matter how much your FOB could use a little more or less of your MO.

These are the four Action Modes and universal instincts Kathy identified in the 1980s. All human beings naturally take action on a continuum of behavior for each of these modes.

Continuum of Behavior in Action Modes

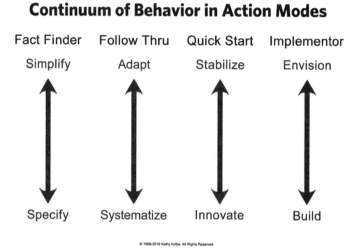

© 1999-2016 Kathy Kolbe. All Rights Reserved.

Fact Finder: *The instinctive way we gather and share information.*
Behavior ranges from gathering detailed information and documenting strategies to simplifying and clarifying options.

Follow Thru: *The instinctive way we organize.*
Behavior ranges from being systematic and structured to being adaptable and flexible.

Quick Start: *The instinctive way we deal with risk and uncertainty.*
Behavior ranges from driving change and innovation to stabilizing and preventing chaos.

Implementor: *The instinctive way we handle space and tangibles.*
Behavior ranges from making things more concrete by building solutions to being more abstract by imagining a solution.

Zones of Operation in the Kolbe Action Modes

You are at your best when you play (or work) in your natural conative zones. The Kolbe Theory specifies three Zones of Operation in each of the four Action Modes measured on a 10-unit scale. Each uses equal amounts of mental energy for creative problem solving and decision making.

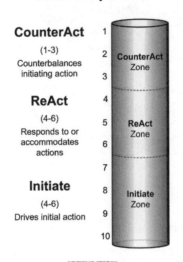

Drew's and Billy's conative realities

Knowing about their differing natural strengths could have prevented the negative outcomes experienced by this father and son.

> Drew Initiates action in Quick Start, which makes him great at speaking spontaneously, being a futurist, and being a risk taker. He resists Follow Thru systems that bog him down in procedures. Individualizing for clients is easy for him. His MO, which showed up on his Kolbe A Index

of conative strengths, is standard for high performers in financial services.

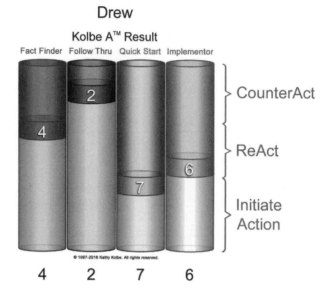

Billy Initiates action in Fact Finder. This helps explain why he was a good student. (From junior high school on, Initiating Fact Finders get the best grades and score highest on the SATs.) He CounterActs in Quick Start, which certainly explains his reticence to deal with the uncertainties of cold calling and his lack of flow when responding to questions.

Billy

Kolbe A™ Result

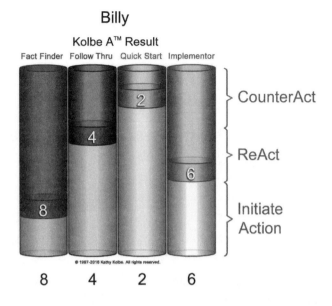

Fact Finder   Follow Thru   Quick Start   Implementor

CounterAct

ReAct

Initiate Action

8   4   2   6

Father and son both ReAct strongly to opportunities in the Implementor mode. That's why they were so comfortable participating in sports and outdoor activities together. It worked well while Billy was growing up, but there was not an outlet for it during the business days when he was struggling and his father kept telling him, "Stop researching about what needs to be done and get out and do it."

Perhaps because Billy did not have his father's conative gift for gab, he had never felt confident getting up in front of people to speak. He describes himself as never having believed in "his abilities" as much as he wished he could. He has plenty of abilities (everyone has an equal amount of conative ability), but they were not valued or praised very often by his father.

All of these issues became clear when the Reality Check results were discussed, but it was too late to prevent the agony they had suffered. Drew had become so disappointed in his son that he lost his temper in front of employees and family on several occasions. That caused him to lose his wife's respect. She felt he was too demanding and authoritarian with their son. As she took her son's side, Drew told her she was the cause of their son's lack of asserting himself. The situation brought out the worst in their relationship and they ended up separating.

Billy left the business with even less self-confidence—and no financial security. Drew did not have the person he had hoped would take over the business. He had also lost considerable respect from his employees and a great deal of money because the distraction reduced his productivity. His greatest regret was losing the companionship of both his wife and his son.

The FM Reality Check for this family business told the members that

- Drew had unrealistic requirements for Billy in the role of future partner in his financial services firm.

- Billy had unrealistic self-expectations for his probable level of success as a future partner in the family financial services firm.

Far better outcomes are seen every time a wannabe FM is a good conative fit for roles that need to be filled in the business.

Reality Checks: Questions to ask yourself

✓ Have the family members in your business carefully considered the consequences if they do not perform well in the company?

✓ Does your FOB build on the conative strengths of all its employees?

✓ Do FMs get involved in your business for the right reasons?

✓ Are all three mental factors (thinking, feeling, doing, or cognitive, affective, conative) recognized for their importance to the FOB?

✓ Are FMs held to the same professional standards as NFMs?

CHAPTER 2

Protecting Values: Keeping Tabs on the Truth

Are you familiar with what we call "billable vacations"? An extraordinarily successful partner in an FOB professional firm confided in us that she and her husband had found "a neat way of double-dipping on billable hours for clients" when they traveled together. Her idea was not original. We're well aware of many of the ways some FOBs try to "play the game."

We're also aware of how easily businesses and the families become the losers.

It's a lot easier to keep tabs on the truth.

Lies hide in sneaky places. When it's your spouse or grandkid who discovers them, it's often "Game Over," and you'll never get a do over.

Your values are either an asset or a liability.

FOBs tend to be more sustainable than your average start-up if the values of the founder are clearly stated and they drive the mission and decision making within the company.

We define business values as conscious judgments or imperatives that deal with what ought to be done. Based on

virtues, business values are a code of honor that pertains to
ethics and that leads to obligations.

Values relate to desires, preferences, and goals. Values are not the
"what" or the "how"; values are the "why."

Among our vast variety of clients, we've seen that those who are
leaders of FOBs often feel they are "doing the right thing" when
their values are tied to their mission. Non-FOB clients rarely talk in
these terms.

Decision making is a lot easier for people in any organization when
there is alignment between what they want to have happen and how
they make it happen. Decisions in any business become very difficult
when you say one thing and do another. If you're in an FOB and
you're an FM, you're going to be scrutinized to see how you practice
the values you preach. That's just the deal.

What values are deal makers—or breakers?

FMs usually assume that they know each other's values and how those
values apply to the goals of the business. Business is Business, however, and the values in some FOBs (like the Mafia), are intentionally
kept quite separate from home and hearth. Going to church with
family and celebrating holidays with them may not predict their business values.

Obviously, not all members of a family share all the same values or
keep tabs on the same truths. Many families have members who support different political candidates. But the FMs who join each other
in a business need to have common convictions and be willing to take
actions that support their beliefs.

Some people start a business as a hobby, and it grows into an
FOB. Others get involved and build it together, which becomes a
family value.

"What we sell is a nonessential thing," a founder told us, "but it has given us a great lifestyle. It does no harm. So we sleep well at night. We travel a lot. We give to charities. We have fun working together. But we don't pretend that if we went out of business, anyone would miss us."

For him, Business is Business. Their shared value is that they keep it simple.

If one FM supports a presidential candidate whose economic policy would directly harm the business, other FMs would rightfully question whether that person (a) doesn't understand the issue or how it would harm the business; (b) doesn't care that it would harm the business; or (c) has concerns he or she considers more important than the impact on the business.

Most people would say it is wrong to take money that is not yours. But ask family, friends, or coworkers to honestly answer what they would do if the change they were handed at a grocery store included an extra $10, and you might be surprised—even shocked—by how many would keep it.

Here's how a difference in values affected one of our clients whose son, Henry, had difficulty finding a job suited to him when he graduated from a college and was deep in debt with student loans. His parents told him he could not live in their home if he wasn't working.

"I'll help you out in the business until I find something that is on the career path I'm looking for," Henry said to his parents, who were partners in a national consulting company.

There were plenty of warning signs for his parents. Although Henry expressed a shared value in the mission of the business, he didn't promise to work as hard as they worked to help the business fulfill its mission. He actually admitted he had no intention of sticking around. They just didn't want to accept it.

Sidestepping all their usual hiring practices, they told their management team that Henry was coming on board to conduct a special research project. They didn't discuss a timeline or budget for it because they had not set specific limits with him.

We got involved two years later when Henry's mother asked us to help them reduce high turnover and low levels of "work ethic" among their employees.

"Something has happened," she said. "We used to have a very loyal team of people who had worked with us for years. We need to get that spirit back in the company."

You know where this is going. How could they not have seen it?

- Henry spent money from profits made by others' efforts. Senior managers had budgeted those profits for bonuses and development of their future projects.

- Henry had overspent and underproduced without limits that would have been set for other employees. His parents had feared that demanding details from him would harm their relationship with Henry. In front of his father, he admitted to us that he never did any of the research his parents thought he was doing. In addition, it was clear to other NFMs that he didn't have the work ethic that was expected of everyone else at the company.

- Henry's father told us that his wife "desperately wanted this to work, and I kind of knew if I got in Henry's way, I would be blamed for his failures."

If Henry had shared his parents' business values, he would not have misspent important resources or burdened them with his employment problem in the first place.

When you want to believe something, and a relative is telling you it's true, you may be tempted to buy into what would sound unrealistic coming from anyone else. Just think about all the Bernie Madoffs who have taken FMs down with them.

FOB leaders need to be aware of FMs who aren't on the same page as everyone else and the possible consequences to the business and family dynamics.

Family and friends often join FOBs because they share the same values. These values become the principles by which the business functions, and disagreements over strategies and tactics remain respectful because both parties can trust each other's motives and goals.

Clarity and consistency between right and wrong make at least some decisions more obvious, even when difficult. It would have been easier if they had been keeping tabs on the truth.

When values collide

What would you do if you were in a position that made you choose between the unanimous recommendation of a group of trusted advisors and your values? Here's how Kathy dealt with it.

> Several years ago I formed an advisory board to help me plan for the succession of my FOB. I had gone from being an entrepreneur with no family members in my company to having my husband and two of my five kids in the business.
>
> The advisory board was made up of very wise, experienced corporate leaders and financial experts. They are people I like, respect, and trust. I met with them to seek their opinion about a succession plan in which my son David

Kolbe and my stepdaughter Amy Bruske would become CEO and president of Kolbe Corp.

Members of the advisory board unanimously recommended against passing the baton to them, despite their being highly qualified. They told me it was because of David's and Amy's values.

Yes, you read that right. They thought David and Amy had the wrong values for serving as leaders in the business I founded.

One advisor said, "Kathy, if you had not spent so much time and energy with your kids and grandkids, this business would easily be ten times bigger. Your kids will make the same mistake."

Another board member said, "If you don't want to keep your work one of the world's best kept secrets, you have to bring in people who won't be limited by doing the same thing you have done—putting their families first."

And another chimed in, "We asked David and Amy, separately, about their personal values, and each said that they valued their family relationships and parenting responsibilities more than creating wealth. This company needs leadership that will focus the energy on the business, not the family."

Clearly, David, Amy, and I have shared values—on many levels.

I promoted David to CEO and Amy to president. I have never regretted that decision.

(I have remained friends with the advisors, but discontinued the advisory board.)

One of the beauties of being a business founder and owner is you are free to make this type of decision. What for many would have been a tough decision was easy for Kathy because of the clarity of the values she shared with her business's FMs.

Get a clue. Ways to assess values.

Want a simple way to assess potential employees' values? Ask questions like the ones that follow before you bring an FM into your business. It is important to clarify the values of the FMs that could influence the business. Their actions—and reactions based upon them—will influence the tone for the company and profoundly affect business decisions.

Questions like these can provide pretty good clues as to the values that are driving an FOB's decisions at any given time in its development:

- **How are your unique business *values* introduced into the FOB?** This implies a separation of business from family values and an open accounting of them. If there is no answer for this there are likely no clear definitions of those values.

- **What value-driven behaviors make the company feel like a family business to employees and customers?** If it is the friendly welcome, that's good. If it is the segregation between family leaders and other employees, that's obviously bad.

- **What's a recent example of how the founder's *values* impacted a business decision?** Cutting family pay more than other employees' pay during tough times says a lot.

- **How and when do FMs interact with NFM employees outside of business hours?** Some FMs stick together in social situations rather than interact with others. They value familial exclusivity. You can bet that NFMs pay attention to signs of an "exclusive club" for family—and maybe just a few highly trusted others.

- **How does the FOB celebrate business achievements?** One would hope that the family includes all employees when celebrating company achievements. Yet, we see FMs save the champagne for special moments with the family only.

- **Do FMs feel it's necessary or desirable to personally use the product or service the business sells?** If FMs don't use what they create why would anyone else believe in the product enough to sell it?

- **Do FMs and NFMs get equal opportunities for bonuses and other benefits?** If not, it's clear NFMs are not as valued. For instance, if FMs are the only employees allowed to travel first class on business trips, others know the family will come first on other benefits too.

Practice what you preach

Beware of posting *values* statements on a wall—unless you are certain you can live up to them. More than anyone, FMs need to act according to those shared values. FMs must be held accountable to the shared values, and while you would hope NFMs do too, the consequences aren't as dire.

As a leader of an FOB, you need to apply your values consistently even though it's not always easy. Remember, in the end it will foster employee loyalty and help you build a better team, one that easily combines family and nonfamily employees.

One of our software development clients asserted that family came first when their son, a company vice president, took paternity leave. Consistently acting on that value was

> soon put to the test: While they were on deadline for a product launch, an NFM project-lead was absent to join his wife for multiple fertility appointments. In spite of the time crunch, we coached the owners to approve the time off or face the consequences of their hypocrisy. Years later, the NFM employee was a vice president himself and one of the most productive leaders in the company.

NFMs will hear your actions far louder than your words. An NFM in an FOB told us he feels like a member of the family, and he tells the people he interviews for jobs that if they ever violate the company work ethic, he will personally escort them out the door. That trumps any poster.

Why would ambitious NFMs want to work for your FOB? Because you make wise business decisions that do not violate your family values or their own, and your values are not in conflict with their values. They also have to believe that you apply your values to situations that involve NFMs just as you do for FMs.

Discussions of values are touchy in job interviews, and even among NFMs after they are hired. Yet strong, shared values often keep people working together even when they disagree significantly on everyday management or financial issues.

When imposing personal values is inappropriate

Business is Business, and there are definite limits on imposing your family values on other employees.

Family values sometimes arise from cultural or religious values, which may or may not translate into business values. The law can guide you in this regard . . . some of the time. There are so many gray areas, however, that time and effort for understanding the reality of how an FOB upholds its values is well spent. That is true for both FMs and NFMs.

It is helpful to get perspective from NFMs or objective advisors in order to avoid the following:

- Insulting any employee's personal values. Example: Allowing sarcastic comments about how employees spend their money.

- Giving business rewards or opportunities to employees based on shared *values* over work performance. Example: Giving extra days off to an employee who works in a nonprofit agency on the weekend but not to an employee who spends the weekend taking care of his own kids.

There are some other gray areas you may need to address:

- Interfering with NFMs' freedom to act according to their differing but appropriate workplace *values*. Example: How will you handle breast-feeding in the office?

- Expressing any value that could seem to be biased toward or against any religion, race, age, or culture. Example: Beginning or ending meetings with prayer.

Personal values, even of the founder, may not always be reflected in the mission or purpose of an FOB. The founder may draft a very clear business mission statement, but it rarely contains a clear statement of his or her *personal values*.

When leaders of an FOB have a conflict between personal values and the company mission, that dissonance reverberates throughout the company. People notice the double standards. Saying one thing in your personal lives, but doing things differently in business, can lead to isolation or termination for an individual. In an FOB it can destroy the business.

A core value for our family is our belief in building on each other's instinctive strengths as well as giving each other the freedom to use them for shared purposes.

We are fortunate to know who we are and to appreciate the differences among us. As you will see from some of the stories we share in this book, our knowledge of what makes each one of us do things the way we do them has helped both of us make wiser decisions and work together and with Kathy's husband (Amy's dad) and Kathy's son (Amy's stepbrother.)

Applying this experience and focusing on conative realities has enabled us to make a bigger difference than if we had focused on financial or skills-based issues.

In the end, success has been tied to people finding the freedom to act on their conative strengths.

When values create competing commitments

You may have been committed, as a family, to some traditional products, policies, or customers that are no longer profitable or wise for you to attempt to accommodate in the future. One of the most important questions to ask annually in any business—especially an FOB—is

What are you NOT going to do in the coming year?

In most businesses, your commitments are to current employees, investors, and customers. In an FOB, you usually have to consider spoken and unspoken commitments to FMs from the past, present, and future too. Every business has to deal with competing commitments, but in an FOB it can become much more complex.

> A family partnership had done pro bono work for three major charities in their community. An NFM asked why they

were doing that instead of hiring more support personnel to help their overworked team. It forced them to weigh pros and cons they had not discussed for years. Family pride of ownership, and of keeping a commitment to the community, had to be compared to their commitment to people who worked for them.

"Grandpa would have said that our employees have the resources to deal with waiting until they get more compensation," one FM said. "The programs we support will have to turn some people away without our contributions."

"Yes, we can also honor Grandpa by sustaining the strong partnership he started," said another FM.

"If we weren't a family business, I'll bet we would all be recommending cutting back on the pro bono work until we're running the partnership more efficiently and can afford to do it again," said a third FM.

The reality of competing commitments in an FOB can become overwhelming because emotions and loyalties are involved. Sometimes these stem from the vision of the next generation of FMs.

Dreams are usually hard to put into words, and they're even harder to achieve over generations in an FOB. When a founder's dream comes close to being a reality, the reality may not look quite so wonderful to other FMs: They may dream bigger dreams or have different visions for their futures.

Ned was an avid cyclist, and his passion grew when he joined a cycle club. He found that he had a knack for repairing the bikes and helping others do the same.

His hobby grew into a small bike repair shop frequented by his fellow cyclists. Word of mouth kept steady business coming through the door and paid the bills . . . and Ned loved tinkering with the bikes all day.

Ned's daughter Ann didn't have the natural ability to repair the bikes; her vision was to grow the business by adding other services and merchandise, such as energy bars, nutrition drinks, new bicycles, and, ultimately, sponsoring cycling events.

By the time Ned was ready to retire, the business had evolved into one with new bike and merchandise sales that seriously outpaced the repair work, which barely made a dent in the revenue.

Ned supported his daughter's vision while he kept doing what he loved, fixing bicycles. One didn't need to fail for the other to succeed.

There are no cookie-cutter solutions to such deeply rooted issues; that's why continuously revisiting values is critical. When you are faced with competing commitments, you need to be flexible enough to reprioritize them. Sometimes you may need to break from tradition or chart a new course.

Reality Checks: Questions to ask yourself

- ✓ What values are deal breakers for FMs?
- ✓ Are any deal breakers not as important for NFMs?
- ✓ How and when are your business values communicated?
- ✓ How is your organization handling a violation of these values for FMs and NFMs?
- ✓ Have clashes in values interfered with productivity?

CHAPTER 3

How Hard Should You Work?

Some things just aren't worth the effort.

Who's to say what those are?

Some things are worth canceling your vacation.

What price will you pay for that?

FMs are likely to push each other to much higher levels of effort more consistently than happens among employees in other businesses. That level of energy can easily transfer to NFMs in the family business, making the entire organization move at a pace rarely seen in other enterprises.

Anyone who doesn't give an FOB a high enough level of effort lowers that collective energy flow in the company. Don't be that person.

Yet FMs can often be heard warning each other to "take a breath" or "slow down before you fall down."

The challenge of working in an FOB is balancing the drive it takes to produce with the need to protect personal and personnel wellness.

There's the "I'll give it a try" level of effort.

Then there's the "It's over my dead body that we would miss this deadline" level of effort.

FMs often know the level of effort being made by other FMs just by their tone of voice, or the pace at which they're talking, or "that look." It takes time to learn that about other people when you begin working with them.

What price do FOBs pay for being highly productive?

Harvard experts note the high productivity in FOBs, estimating that they account for about 66 percent of all businesses around the globe,[1] yet FOBs provide 70 to 90 percent of the global GDP[2] or productive results. It's not surprising to us that FOBs are often much more productive than publicly financed corporations. From what we have observed they are also more likely to donate time and talent to philanthropic activities.

That which makes FOBs so able to do all this can also make them set a cruel pace. Consistently high expectations can lead to a frenzy of effort that becomes impossible to sustain. That's when FMs will benefit from knowing how to *Do Nothing*—because, otherwise, nothing will work.

Safety experts have taken teeter-totters out of playgrounds. In an FOB, however, no one protects players involved in the jarring teeter-totter effect that requires balancing levels of effort with the need to occasionally drop the effort and Do Nothing.

This chapter will give you some ground rules to help you keep the fun of the teeter-totter in play while also keeping it in balance. Everyone has to keep up their own end. It starts when you get on board. All FMs and NFMs need to ask themselves

---

1 Harvard Business School, Interview with John Davis, accessed July 30, 2016, http://www.exed.hbs.edu/assets/Pages/video.aspx?videoid=48.

2 Family Firm Institute, "Global Data Points," accessed July 30 2016, http://www.ffi.org/page/globaldatapoints.

- Do I have a high enough level of commitment to the FOB that I will give up other opportunities to do the work it requires?

- Am I willing and able to put forth the effort to learn all that I need in order to make wise decisions on behalf of the business?

FOBs need to make sure job candidates know that their expected levels of effort are potentially higher than they've experienced in other places. Being forewarned removes a lot of angst. New employees can tell their spouses that they'll probably be home later for dinner when projects are on deadline.

Our Dynamynd Interview process (see the Selected Kolbe Products and Services at the back of the book for more information) provides questions you can ask job candidates to assess demonstrated levels of effort. It brings objectivity to your discussion when you want to hire your cousin but your instincts are holding you back.

As an example, you might ask "What work-related projects have taken a lot of persistent effort, and how did you contribute to their success?"

We also advise that FOBs lean toward hiring NFMs who have formerly worked in FOBs or grown up in them. Others might think they understand how family enterprises differ from other businesses. Being immersed in an FOB prepares you better for realities and how to live through similar situations.

> Yuko was totally intrigued by the job description given her by the HR manager at a high-tech FOB. But when the topic turned to warning her how an FOB works, Yuko waved off the HR manager and said, "I get it."
>
> "I grew up in a family business," Yuko explained. "It means every single minute must be used productively. You

watch what family members do. If they take short breaks,
you take short breaks. If they change paths, you adjust
to the new direction. And when you have big successes,
there's lots and lots of hugging."

Yuko got the job over two other equally qualified candidates.

Making an attempt is not good enough

A professional sports team is not going to win games if some of the
players are just making attempts and are not at the commitment level
or beyond. It'll show up in the first quarter of a basketball game. The
coach or teammates will have to pressure the slackers to step up their
game; otherwise, it's "game over."

Fans also try to be the extra player (the *sixth man* on a basketball
team) to make them lift their game. Sometimes that actually works.
The most important differences, however, are made when individual
players drop their petty attitudes, stop making mere attempts, and
bring their best game to the effort.

Just as Charles Barkley, by showboating rather than driving toward
the basket, lowered his teammates' game, so does an FM let all other
FMs down when he or she goofs off. We suggest benching players
in the FOB if they are unwilling to function at high levels of commitment. Their level of effort has nothing to do with their capabilities and everything to do with the personally determined use of their
abilities.

Recognize your value to the company. Clarify your purposes for
being there. But, ultimately, the differences you make also require
that you make a higher level of effort in all three mental factors.

At the very least, FMs and NFMs need to renew their commitment to the business annually by asking each other these questions:

• What do we want to have happen?

- Do all of us share purposes and agree on the paths necessary to achieve them?

- Do we have the right mix of natural abilities to do what we need to do?

- Are we finding joy in what we are doing?

- Are we making the differences in the world that we set out to make?

What's in it for you?

Working in an FOB requires giving up other opportunities, including what would be considered personal time off in most other businesses. NFMs may not have to give up quite as much, but they also need to recognize that a commitment to an FOB is a commitment to a cause.

Contrary to suspicions that many NFMs have about FOBs, we've found only a few greedy FOB leaders who make a higher salary than a comparable NFM employee does. Many FMs could make as much, or more, money if they weren't tied to the FOB. Those who believe they could not do so pay the price of never knowing if that is actually true. Sure, there are some tax benefits and more flexible work hours, but the ratio of those benefits to pay-per-effort is lopsided in most companies with which we work. Frankly, when that's not the case, we are unlikely to continue to keep them as clients.

If you don't care much about what the business does, or the customers/clients you do it for, or even for the people who do it, then it makes little sense for you to be involved in an FOB, either as an FM, an NFM, or a consultant.

Be honest with yourself and others about the levels of effort that are sustainable for you to contribute to an FOB. You and it will both suffer if the business uses scarce resources to develop your abilities, only to have you decide to use them outside the company.

A simple question can put this issue on the table:

Is being in the FOB a *job* for you,
or is it your long-term *career?*

Being an FM in an FOB is often a 24/7 commitment. Are you willing to be the FM who has to get to the office fast if the fire department calls, who has to deal with an employee who is injured, who has to pick up a customer who flies in for an urgent meeting, or who has to take out the trash when it's overflowing?

If you would not volunteer in any of these situations, perhaps you ought not to be in the FOB. If you would only be willing to do these things until something better comes along, be very sure that is understood by the other FMs in the business. Lack of understanding on this matter can have unfortunate repercussions in family relationships.

"Do what needs to get done, or get out" is the often unspoken truth in an FOB.

We once had an NFM employee quit her job at Kolbe Corp because, she said, "There's no place to hide here. Everyone expects everyone else to work all day long. The only time I feel free to call a friend is when I'm on break." To which we shrugged and wondered, "Why would she expect anything else?"

Should founders expect FMs to be as committed as they are? They'd better be, or they ought not to be there. To take over leadership requires a high level of effort. It requires empathetic and visionary leadership that is important in any type of business.

It may be wishful thinking on our part, but we have seen considerably more leaders who give a top level of effort in FOBs than in public companies or government. For businesses that pride themselves on being concerned about social responsibility, as is true of most FOBs, it's not just about having a passion; it's about compassion for employees and about commitment to the mission of the company.

To our dismay, we have not consistently seen that compassion and commitment in the leadership of nonprofit organizations. It seems many nonprofit board members are there to beef up their vitae more than to keep the enterprise sustainable. Nonprofit private schools with fabulous programs for kids have had to shut down because board members did not watch the budget closely enough. Fund-raising golf tournaments sponsored by hospital foundations have given less than 8 percent of the proceeds to the hospital.

On the government side, far more conative energy is spent getting elected than serving in office. Once elected, the efforts seem more devoted to being reelected than to any other purpose.

The nice thing about an FOB is that you don't have to campaign for the job, you get reelected daily, and the money stays in the family.

Managing mental energy

You don't have an unlimited amount of conative energy. You have the same amount as every other human being. And, like everyone else, when you exhaust it, you'll have to replace it.

Unfortunately, most people pay more attention to recharging their cell phones than to recharging their brainpower.

You can't just plug your brain into an external drive. The only way to get it back up to speed is to get downtime. Sleep is the most effective method. You can't do that on the job, but you can—and should—take mental breaks to let your brain reenergize.

Kathy discovered the nature of the smallest units of this mental factor, so she got to name them. She chose the term "ergs," since they are a natural source of energy, and scientists use "erg" to describe the smallest unit of physical energy. (For you Scrabble players out there, you're welcome.)

Most people have a pretty full tank of mental energy when they wake up from a full night's sleep. (We haven't any idea how much mental energy nightmares use up.) Why do some people feel more mentally alert than others do?

"I wake up almost in a brain fog most weekdays, and it gets worse as the day goes on," Antonio said. "My brother tells

me that he bounds out of bed with ideas on his mind. I'm
jealous of him for that."

It's a good bet that his brother, Carlo, loves his job in the FOB.

"Yep, Carlo is doing exactly what he should be doing. He
even says he would never want to be doing anything else.
I am trying to fill the role of chief financial officer because
that's what I went to school to learn to do, but I actually
hate having to do it. It just goes against my instincts when I
have to do such nitpicky things."

Why would Antonio bound out of bed to do a job he hates doing?
He wouldn't. Of course, he's dragging even more at the end of the
day. He's working harder than Carlo because he has to push himself
to tackle his daily tasks. Yet he accomplishes less.

Using each and every one of your ergs takes both time and effort.
You burn up conative energy with every mental effort you make. It
takes extra effort to work against your grain. It uses up more ergs,
but you end up with little to show for it. In short, it gives you a poor
return on your effort.

If you drain your ergs but keep trying to work, you will burn
out, mentally. We've seen what researchers have identified as conative energy in the brain slow down while doing studies using qEEG
brain-mapping. It takes a lot of downtime to reenergize (regenerate
ergs) after you do that to yourself.

At the end of the day, Carlo still has ergs he can use to join in
recreational activities with his family. The most Antonio can muster
up is a little energy to watch TV or play computer games—*simple*
computer games.

"So that's why I need more vacations these days. When I was in a groove, doing work that fit me perfectly, it was like being in a glide pattern," Antonio said. "I didn't even take all the vacation time I had because I was energized by my work. Now my resistant Follow Thru loves anything and everything that interrupts the work I should be doing."

Antonio's entire team is suffering along with him.

"It brings us all down to have to wait for Antonio to approve reports," his financial analyst said. "None of us can move forward without his direction. He's the FM guy who needs to make decisions. When he is indecisive, it affects all of us. I find myself getting frustrated, and the work is more laborious than I ever remember it being."

What both Antonio and Carlo needed was to understand the specifics of their differing MOs and how those natural conative abilities fit their roles in the business. Providing this information is simple and straightforward for us—and we love being able to do it. The next section explains why we were able to do what Antonio, Carlo, and so many others refer to as our having "changed [their] lives."

Branding by Action Modes

When truly striving (not just going through the motions), people will take action with the inborn pattern of behaviors that characterizes them—their MO. That MO kicks in the moment they decide to make a commitment to getting something done.

You, like all other human beings, have four conative strengths in your MO; one in each Action Mode. We are who we are, conatively, and the Action Modes through which we Initiate action are our hallmark—and often a big part of our personal brand.

12 Kolbe Strengths

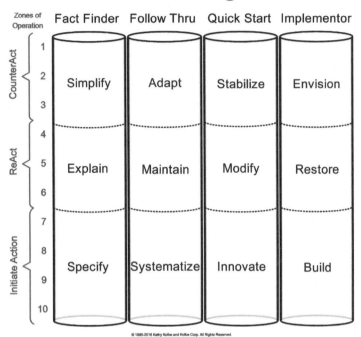

Zones of Operation		Fact Finder	Follow Thru	Quick Start	Implementor
CounterAct	1				
	2	Simplify	Adapt	Stabilize	Envision
	3				
ReAct	4				
	5	Explain	Maintain	Modify	Restore
	6				
Initiate Action	7				
	8	Specify	Systematize	Innovate	Build
	9				
	10				

© 1995-2016 Kathy Kolbe and Kolbe Corp. All Rights Reserved.

What Kathy has dubbed Operating Zones determine the way you use the instincts that drive the Action Modes. For instance, we all organize in some way. As you'll see, the Initiating Follow Thrus are the neatniks, and the CounterAct Follow Thrus are the slobs. You aren't going to change nature, so in an FOB, and at home, you'd better learn to live with it.

INITIATE: HOW YOU BEGIN THE PROBLEM-SOLVING PROCESS

We begin striving on any project through the mode in which we have the most ergs, or the longest line on our Kolbe A Index result. It's not uncommon for people to refer to themselves with a sort of shorthand: "I'm a Quick Start." FMs who know each other well will "get it." Here are some shorthand descriptions for how people Initiate Action in each Action Mode.

Fact Finder: The Researcher

Having an Initiating Fact Finder in the family business is helpful because they naturally

- Prioritize
- Document
- Detect errors and calculate remedies

Count on them to tell you "It depends," when you try to get a quick answer out of them.

Follow Thru: The Organizer

Family businesses benefit greatly when Initiating Follow Thru relatives contribute this knack for

- Structuring systems
- Providing continuity and carrying out themes
- Keeping things tidy and bringing closure

Even if you put something you borrow back exactly where it was, they know it was moved.

Quick Start: The Innovator

Without Initiating Quick Starts, family businesses wouldn't get launched or survive many catastrophes. These FMs

- Improvise
- Handle deadlines with a sense of urgency
- Are natural deal makers

It's never a problem getting ideas from them, but it's tough to get them to stop starting over again.

Implementor: The Protector

Initiating Implementors provide essential quality and safety for a family business by

- Protecting and utilizing property and technology
- Constructing and mechanizing
- Demonstrating solutions

Don't ask them to describe what they're doing; they will show you, not tell you how.

COUNTERACT (AKA RESISTING): HOW YOU RESIST ACTING IN THE PROBLEM-SOLVING PROCESS

There are people with strengths on the opposite end of the continuum in each mode who naturally resist all the Initiatives going in one direction. For them, "enough is enough." So they push back.

These CounterActions have a positive impact in all businesses. We're talking in conative terms here, so there should be no implied negative affect (anger, spite, or cognitive corrections). Pushing back is a natural way to keep momentum going instead of getting bogged down in one way of striving.

CounterActions make as powerful and as intense a contribution to creative problem solving as do Initiating actions.

Most of us have the conative need to CounterAct or resist in at least one Action Mode. You'll see this strength play out in the following ways.

Fact Finder: The Simplifier

The contribution of this strength can be valuable to your FOB by

- Cutting through complexities
- Condensing the documents and agendas
- Summarizing lengthy talking points to bullet points

Follow Thru: The Adaptable

Systems are great, but your business needs people with this drive to take the random route that might lead you to ways that

- Diversify
- Transform
- Bypass bureaucracies

Quick Start: The Stabilizers

Essential to every enterprise is the inclination of some participants to

- Perpetuate
- Retain
- Caution

Implementor: The Envisioner

These are the people who don't need to see it to believe it because they

- Imagine
- Visualize
- Conceptualize

CounterActions, or conative resistances, are productive in nature because they do the following:

- Offer a contrast and give balance to the way action is being taken.
- Present a different point of view.
- Prevent problems when there is too much energy bounding off in one direction.

REACT (AKA ACCOMMODATING): HOW YOU
RESPOND IN THE PROBLEM-SOLVING PROCESS

An FOB has a great need for conative accommodation because working together over time is a highly desired goal for FMs. The push and pull of Initiating behaviors being met head-on by resistant behaviors can cause FMs to take sides with their conative lookalikes. Forming such conative cliques robs a business of joy as well as productivity. Our hope is that this book will help you avoid that.

Accommodating in an Action Mode means using, adding to, or in some way responding to others' conative actions on opposite ends of the continuum. It can include editing a Fact Finder's manuscript, sticking with a Follow Thru's timeline, trying out a Quick Start's innovation, or utilizing the technology center built by an Implementor.

Fortunately there is more accommodation energy in the world than initiation or resistance. While 20 to 25 percent of the conative energy in our huge sample of over 1,500,000 Kolbe A Index results includes both initiation and resistance, 50 to 60 percent of it is in accommodating behaviors.

Remember, every part of an MO is a natural strength. Praise the "neatnik" for being such a great organizer, and be glad your slob can also be a fabulous disruptive innovator.

If both Antonio and Carlo were in roles that made wise use of the conative ergs in each Action Mode, both would be more likely to thrive in their business.

Maximizing conative strengths

FMs need their available mental energy to deal with family issues and with FOB issues. If you are an FM, you may sometimes ask yourself, "How about using some of them just for me?"

You use up conative ergs at work, and you use them for community fund-raising efforts, family outings, bridge tournaments, travel, home repairs, and painting classes. Anything that requires decision making eats up some of your time and energy.

It's easier to allocate that energy between your work and your personal life if you don't have overlapping priorities. That comes with the territory when you work in a family business.

Some people think that working together in an FOB gives you a twofer because you get to be around your family at the same time you are working.

> "I spend lots of time working with Dad" a daughter said,
> "but it's not the same as going fishing with him. There's no
> time for storytelling when we're on deadlines at work."

Dad and daughter work well together because they contribute effort at the same levels.

> "Mom's a different story," she explains. "Mom comes in
> and out of the office, always in a hurry to drop something
> off, or give us an assignment. I don't see her contributing
> much, and it makes me mad. She doesn't mind spending
> the money, but she's not doing much to help us make it.
> It makes me care less about spending any of my free time
> doing anything with her."

Mom and Dad have a deal that their daughter needs to know about. Dad agreed to put all his energy into their business if Mom would put her energy into keeping the home and family activities going. She's in charge of what they call the "FOF," or "family-owned family." (We won't be using that phrase, although we love the way they do.)

She keeps track of their personal finances, handles home maintenance and repairs, the hiring and firing of tradespeople and contractors, and the deal making that goes with it. She also does all the purchasing of supplies, prepares the meals, and plans their vacations. In addition, she stays on top of their personal calendar, including the social, health-related, and entertainment activities. She also has to deal with solicitors—and the cable guy!

Mom uses up all her ergs to support Dad, who is the one-person manager of almost everything that happens in their business. She gives as much effort to her work as do Dad and daughter at the FOB. As is often the case, she is an FM who is not on the payroll but who is critically important to the success of the business.

Regardless of your role in an FOB, the amount of effort you contribute needs to be both recognized and nurtured. People don't contribute their ergs to a cause in which they have little at stake.

Playing with the ball of dirt in your hand

We've learned a lot from little kids. They use their mental energy to do what matters most to them. And they know when to Do Nothing. Our most basic rule for all FMs and NFMs, people whose hard work contributes so much to our GDP, is this: Do Nothing—when Nothing Works.

Here's one of our favorite dialogues with a six-year-old.

> "Sam, what did you do at school today?"
> "Nothing."
> "When did you Do Nothing?"
> "Lots of the time."
> "Why did you Do Nothing?"
> "Just cuz."
> "Where did you Do Nothing?"
> "Everywhere."
> "How do you Do Nothing?"
> "You don't try to do it. You just play with the ball of dirt in your hand."

If you haven't *just played with the ball of dirt* lately, you haven't given your instincts their best chance of helping you make wise decisions. (If you haven't talked about Doing Nothing with a young child, you have missed out on our favorite after-school discussion topic.)

Doing Nothing is what artists do when they stare out the window, or what parents do when they don't agree with a neighbor's criticism of their child. It's what farmers do when they just kick the dirt. It's also what wise employees do when they run out of mental energy.

Don't take doing nothing too literally. It can include these kinds of activities:

- Daydreaming
- Watching stupid TV
- Reading for pure pleasure
- Having idle chats
- Cooking without a cause

It's so logical to Do Nothing—when Nothing Works. Even Oprah, in one of her own books, didn't feel it necessary to attribute it to Kathy's long-standing rule. (See her "5 Rules for Trusting Your Instincts" in the appendix.)

There are plenty of good reasons to trust your instincts, but most people are so unaware of them that they stick with the old standards such as *think before you speak* (which keeps people from saying what they really need to say) and *don't rock the boat* (which leads to lack of innovation).

Those mistakes are made less often in FOBs than other types of businesses. Rather than banning the teeter-totters, they've learned how to get just the right balance between high levels of productivity and just playing with the dirt. By the time FMs are in the business, they have usually had many opportunities to see Sam fidget with dirt while he's coming up with his best ideas.

Reality Checks: Questions to Ask Yourself

- ✓ Do you look forward to doing the work you do?

- ✓ Does the way you work inspire others to do their best?

- ✓ Do you show appropriate respect for the work relatives do outside the FOB, and NFMs do in the FOB?

- ✓ Are you making conscious decisions about the level of effort you give various activities in your life?

- ✓ Is it wise for you to be (or not to be) an FM in your family business?

CHAPTER 4

Banking on Trust

Building trust is essential to the health of any kind of business. One of the benefits of bringing FMs into an FOB is they usually walk in the door with a certain level of trust already established.

Founders tell us they can sleep a little easier at night when they have a well-trusted FM keeping watch over the company assets. This gives them the peace of mind that allows them to focus on growing the business.

Business is Business. Don't spend your time and energy working at building trust if your instincts tell you a person ought not to be trusted.

We've been there, done that, and regret every legal dollar it has cost to later correct the problems that resulted.

The golden rule: Trust your instincts

To follow this golden rule in an FOB, you first have to trust your own instincts, then the instincts of other FMs, and those of NFMs.

This instinctive trust, especially as it relates to problem solving, simplifies communication, defines roles, and helps determine objectively who should work together.

Rules for trusting your instincts are an oxymoron. Instincts are precognitive drives. They are the "Just do it" factor. Why the need for rules for using what comes naturally?

Chalk it up to having it pounded into our heads that we are stupid if we don't "Think before you speak." Even a *Wiki* article that lists 10 steps for thinking before you speak begins with this caveat: "It would clearly be undesirable for us to have to formulate our thoughts before issuing an immediate warning '*run!*'"[3]

Just as the existence of conation itself has been ignored by academics, so has any approach to problem solving that does not both begin and end in the cognitive domain.

Instincts are the inborn, natural drives that give you the mental energy to do something about your desires. They differ from intuition, which is an affective feeling that engages your instincts to take action. Since instincts compel you to create solutions according to an innate pattern of getting things done, they click in ahead of conscious thought. Were that not true, we would have no heroes. Who would be able to jump in front of the train to save the infant? Not the person thinking about the odds of survival; instead, the person who trusts his or her instincts just does it.

If you don't trust your own instincts, why would anyone else?

Waiting to act until you have a meeting of the minds is like asking Superman to wait until he's facilitated a town hall meeting before he swoops in to save the city.

If you don't trust your instincts, don't get into an FOB. That's because your instincts will be your go-to source of power. We aren't talking about the affectively driven kind such as maternal "instincts" or fight-or-flight "instincts"; this is the *real-deal* power—the measurable conative resource within you. It can be the difference between surviving and failing in a crisis.

---

3   "How to Think Before Speaking," WikiHow, accessed July 30, 2016, http://www.wikihow.com/Think-Before-Speaking.

Trusting your own instincts, or conative MO, above others' needs is like putting the oxygen mask over your face on an airplane before putting it on a person next to you. If you can't read your instincts, you aren't in a position to help others use or benefit from theirs.

While it's critical to develop a high level of trust in others in an FOB, it's not a panacea. You can't sit back and delegate your decisions to others just because you trust them. Nor can you ignore what your gut is telling you to do in favor of seeking consensus among all your trusted FMs. In certain situations, blindly trusting other FMs can lead you down the wrong path. To avoid this outcome, learn to trust your instincts even when they may run counter to what other FMs are advising.

Do a gut check

Here's a quick check you can use to see how often you trust your gut instincts without hesitation.

On a scale of 1–5, with 5 being *very often*, and 1 being *rarely*, circle how often you

		RARELY . . . VERY OFTEN				
1.	Wait until you're sure.	1	2	3	4	5
2.	Just do it.	1	2	3	4	5
3.	See what others think.	1	2	3	4	5
4.	See what happens.	1	2	3	4	5
5.	Consider the consequences.	1	2	3	4	5
6.	Go out on a limb.	1	2	3	4	5
7.	Recall how it has worked best.	1	2	3	4	5
8.	Do it off the top of your head.	1	2	3	4	5
9.	Make sure you are right.	1	2	3	4	5
10.	Play a hunch.	1	2	3	4	5

Total the circled numbers for the even-numbered questions. Then total the circled numbers for the odd-numbered ones. Deduct the odd number total from the even number total. If you don't end up with a positive number, then you are not trusting your gut.

_____   –   _____   =   _____
    Even numbers   Odd numbers   Total number

As you probably guessed, the odd-numbered questions are about how you perform when you think before you act. The even-numbered ones relate to ways you can Act before You Think (See the appendix, "5 Rules for Trusting Your Instincts").

A Follow Thru Initiator may stop to straighten items on his desk before evacuating when the fire alarm goes off. If your instincts tell you to run, then run!

If a CounterActing Fact Finder believes you have enough information to be able to make a big decision, but your instincts tell you to look more deeply into the data, stop and dig deeper.

When FMs are involved, you'll find it tough NOT to listen to their input. We have seen highly functioning leaders yield to "family decisions" rather than trusting themselves. Getting everyone to agree on a process is a fool's journey.

> We learned a great deal from Rich, a long-term client of ours. He founded a business 35 years ago as a spin-off of a company his parents had run for years. He learned to work hard, persevere, be smart with money, and respect the talents of his employees. He also knew the importance of trust.
>
> Rich made it clear that one of the big benefits of bringing in FMs was the ability to trust them with money and to protect the brand ("At least most family members," he was quick to point out).

> We soon realized that Rich also tended to trust others'
> instincts more than he trusted his own. He leaned on us too
> heavily when considering development of new products. It
> would have been easy for us to say, "Go for it. You have the
> right team in place to do it. They've bought into the proj-
> ect and they have the strengths to do it." But that would
> have been wrong for us to say. A big part of our role was to
> help him develop confidence by learning to trust his own
> instincts in the decision-making process.

With all the wisdom Rich has brought to his business, we found it disheartening to hear him ask his managers about their hunches regarding deals—especially because he asked before checking his own gut reactions.

It's often tempting to lean on the MO of other FMs rather than trying to decipher your own reactions. It's easy to say "Just do it" to someone else, when it's you yourself who should be calling the shots.

We have observed many people in leadership roles whose indecisiveness is due to their lack of trust in their own instincts. Their usual trick is to try to get the team they are supposedly leading to reach a consensus on issues. While this is a method of getting "buy-in," it is often a time-consuming cop-out.

> "In a way, it was easier to just do what everyone agreed we
> should do," Rich told us. "But once you taught me to get away
> from all the 'shoulds,' I went from controlling from the rear
> to leading the entire team (family and all) from up front."

Business is Business, and decision makers who worry too much about FMs' feelings not only are in danger of denying their own instincts; they often also lose their cognitive objectivity. Business relationships based on emotional connections detract from the objectivity necessary for everything from performance reviews to developing business strategies.

The power of knowing FMs' instinct-based truths

Camaraderie develops among cohorts who trust one another's instincts. It allows a freedom of action and openness to be yourself. It's the stuff of great buddy movies.

Mutual and unconditional trusting of instincts among players leads to a closeness that spans years, distance, and other differences. Those who experience it in the military, in sports, or in putting together a high school musical will always have a special bond. It is no different for FMs who work together.

Parents and children have years together in which to develop trust in each other. In a good parent-child relationship, kids know that the parent will be there and take care of them. They count on being picked up on time, dropped off on time, and not having to worry about anything because they know their parents will make sure that their needs are met. That's the very foundation of these relationships—even when the children become teenagers.

As kids seek more independence, they have to prove that they can be trusted with everything from making wise shopping decisions to driving a car safely. After going through all these "tests," they enter FOBs as young adults (or any age) and may have to pass trust tests again in that business setting.

FMs have an advantage because they have had personal situations in which they experienced the power of one another's instincts. This can be a two-edged sword, though. Brothers and sisters have had their fights and learned what they can trust about each other. They also know how to push each other's buttons to get the results the company needs:

- "I can get my brother to buckle down just by giving him shorter deadlines."

- "My sister can't live with a mess, so I know she'll clean up that flow chart no matter how long it takes."

Trusting a marriage partner you work with involves all three mental factors—thinking (cognitive), feeling (affective), and doing (conative). At home, the relationship is far more affective, meaning you love them and trust their values. That doesn't mean they have the right cognitive and conative makeup to work together, for example,

- A woman loves her husband and trusts him around the house, but his natural CounterAction in Implementor mode doesn't lend itself to handling space and facilities.

- A husband loves his wife and trusts her with money, but her natural CounterAction in Follow Thru doesn't fit with having to go through the process of reconciling the books to the penny.

Drawing false conclusions

Beware of drawing conclusions about an FM's natural abilities. Just because you're married does not mean you know how your spouse will function in a work environment. Most personal relationships do not involve striving behaviors so much as they involve emotions. Love can blind you to how the other person handles a crisis. Until you have been through a few of those together, you may not know the other's realities.

Your guesses about a sibling's MO are likely to be more accurate than those about your spouse. You probably had to cut a lot of deals with the sibling over sharing spaces and stuff, time, and attention. Your sibling's kid is an entirely different situation.

Since our research shows that instincts are not passed down to the next generation, your nephew may be nothing like your sister in the way he takes action. If you have not been around him when he has been free to solve problems in his own way, you don't have much more of a basis for knowing how he will perform than you do regarding any other new hire.

Don't count on family stories for insights into how an FM will perform. They are often filled with a range of myths and stereotypes—including his being the golden boy or perhaps being dinged for coming in last in the 5th grade melon-eating contest.

Carefully consider their Kolbe A Index results before giving relatives a role or judging their contributions. Don't set them up for failure because of fourth-hand stories or others misleading you about their strengths.

Here's how it happens in the workplace. You might think it is appropriate to ask nephew Harry to do the research and fact finding for a project without realizing that his instincts make him a guy who will bring you a bunch of bullet points, without much detail. That's who he is. If that's the way you want the information delivered, he's your guy. If not, you have set him up for failure.

All too often, people think they can trust people because they know their high levels of interest and of skills. Yes, those are important considerations. But, in the end, it's not about what you want to do or can do; it's about what you will do, which is conative. It *is* trusting that the person you live with will put the spices back in the right place or that the person you work with will be open to making some changes in a team. That trust has to be based on realities.

> Knowing Harriet has the instincts to make all the plans for the company strategic-planning retreat doesn't mean she will use those instincts for that task. Why might she not be the right person for a job even though it suits her instincts?
>
> • She may not choose to use her instincts for a job she doesn't want to do.
>
> • She may have used up all the energy she would need to do it.

- She may have a conative conflict, or her approach may differ from the cochair's—so, they would waste time and effort arguing over the process.

- She may have no experience doing this type of thing.

Trusting people to do what they do well is easier said than done, because you need to consider all these other factors. It would seem that you should have a better handle on how much you can trust an FM to get the job done. Yet, you may not. You may feel Harriet let you down, but you had unrealistic expectations. Maybe you didn't know about her other assignments or think about the conflict she was experiencing.

If you don't know the instinctive truths about people, it's difficult to predict their actions. Assuming they will do what you want them to do can lead to false hopes or unmet expectations.

To turn this around, FOBs must invest in learning to understand, respect, and provide their people with the freedom to use their instincts. It's tough to do this if you have never even considered that instincts matter.

Don't hire FMs if you wouldn't trust them in a crisis

This is what we affectionately refer to as the "if-you-wouldn't-let-her-help-you-with-your-wedding-don't-work-with-her rule."

If you frequently felt that your daughter was faking a headache to get out of dealing with a troubling matter, or your son wasn't fessing up when he was the cause of an accident, remember this: Business is Business, and you won't be able either to cover for your kids or to persuade other employees to think such behavior is acceptable.

If an FM is not trustworthy in personal settings there is no way you should put yourself in the position of trusting him or her at work. Case in point:

> Having founded a nonprofit community health program decades earlier, the CEO had hired dozens of employees, placed them in roles, trained them, and managed their performance. She felt good about her ability to handle a wide variety of situations, so was confident that she would be able to bring her daughter into the organization at a mid-management level, even though her daughter had less job experience than others hired in similar roles. She trusted her daughter as the single parent of the founder's grandchild, after all.
>
> When her senior management team had an encounter with the founder a couple of years later, one of the reasons they gave for demanding that she retire (the "Or else . . ." was an unstated reality) was that she had not stopped her daughter from misappropriating funds from the organization.
>
> "Damn," she thought to herself, "I thought she learned her lesson when she got in trouble a few years ago for the minor shoplifting episode."
>
> "You lost our trust," they told the founder, "when you showed an inability to protect the company from the inappropriate actions of your daughter."

Any time you can avoid putting an FM in a situation that could influence the outcome negatively, you are saving both the company and the FM from a potential problem. That's when it's really smart to say, "This is not working. I'm not firing you; I'm counseling you"—into either a different role in the FOB or a better situation outside of it.

A situational breach of trust is not going to destroy your family relationship unless it is left unresolved. You can be a generally trustworthy person in terms of your honesty and character. Everyone has some things they should not be counted on to do well.

Worst-case scenarios involve a breach of trust with your corporate mission, its finances, or reputation. Those are obviously deal breakers. An FM may get an extra chance in cases of misplaced situational trust, but there ought never to be a second chance if trust is broken regarding basic values. This is when you have to terminate the FM's employment.

Give NFMs opportunities to earn trust

Rarely can an FOB build a management team with just FMs. It ought to be the goal of any FOB to find and keep employees, both FMs and NFMs, who are worthy of that level of trust and respect. Too many leaders don't realize how they limit the potential of the business when they exclude NFMs from the circle of trust.

When FMs trust the instincts of NFMs, they become like members of the family.

> As with many founders of Internet-based FOBs, Omar is not a proficient programmer. And none of the FMs in his business have technology-related skills. So, Omar relies on Dante, an NFM chief technology officer, to manage the firm's software-based intellectual property and guard all access to the FOB's passwords and accounts. It isn't a matter of giving Dante a dollar limit for purchases. Omar is, in essence, giving him the keys to their kingdom.

Empowering an NFM to make decisions necessary to do such jobs requires unlimited trust. Some FOB consultants will say that no one outside the family should be trusted to that degree. But in this case, Dante earned the trust and, with it, he became much like an FM. Without it, he could not have functioned in his job. Now Omar and other FMs can fully relax, even to the point of being out of the office at the same time. And, they won't be as likely to badger the next generation of FMs into filling that role.

NFMs don't have the advantage of knowing the personal history of FMs, which puts them at a great disadvantage in an FOB. There are no rules that can change that reality. If NFMs are smart, they'll pay attention. By listening to the stories FMs tell, they may glean information that helps them understand how to best build trust with FMs and others within the company. The issue, therefore, is not about the inequality of trust at the get-go; it is the question of whether NFMs in the business are given equal opportunities to earn trust.

If FMs show an inclination to trust only other FMs, or to trust them sooner or more, it could have a highly negative effect on others. The best solution for most issues involving levels of trust is to develop a process that allows NFMs to be in a position to gain trust as soon as possible.

You may be the lowest level FM in the business, and you want to use every opportunity to prove yourself worthy of having been shown trust. Stop a minute, though, to consider that your NFM coworker is struggling just to get *the chance* to *be trusted*.

Share the opportunity. Work collaboratively. As you rise in the organization, you will need cohorts you can trust as teammates. Shining the light on the trustworthiness of your coworker is a way of building his or her trust in you.

Some of the most trustworthy employees we have ever worked with are those who have worked side by side with FMs who vouched for them. This opened doors to opportunities that may otherwise not have been available to them.

What breaks trust?

For both FMs and NFMs, it is the fear of betrayal that interferes with the ability to build trust. When that fear is real—when people in your company are betrayed routinely—it is especially difficult to overcome.

FOBs have a set of ethical issues that aren't present in other businesses. If you recognize the issues, establish guidelines for how to deal with them, and follow those guidelines, they won't be big problems. Here are some of the ethical issues we've identified for which guidelines are essential—and will result in broken trust if they aren't honored.

First are examples of ways we've seen many FMs take unreasonable advantage of other FMs. These things often happen without comment from the victim. The natural negative consequences, however, are likely to surface over time.

Breaking trust with FMs

- Taking advantage of an FM's abilities without giving appropriate compensation

- Requiring FMs to put in considerably more time than others—without prior agreement

- Treating FMs as personal servants

- Expecting FMs to sign documents without asking any questions

- Ridiculing an FM in front of others just to make a point

The next examples may not have such long-term consequences because the NFMs treated in such ways are unlikely to stick around.

Breaking trust with NFMs

- Giving FMs a greater chance to succeed than NFMs

- Overlooking the errors and omissions of FMs, but penalizing NFMs for similar issues

- Using a commissioned person's time to train an FM without compensation

- Allowing an unskilled FM to do harm to the efforts of others

Trust-breakers can kill an FOB, so you need to be alert to these issues and work to prevent them.

To help with these preventative efforts, recognize that the suspicions that lead to a lack of trust are based on attitudes, not necessarily actions. When trust-breaking is endemic in organizations, it usually means that they are failing. If you aren't in a position to fix this problem, then you should get out ASAP, whether you are an FM or an NFM. Working in such an environment is unhealthy for everyone involved.

Breaking trust in an FOB is a painful betrayal

The business is "the baby" to many founders. They protect and nurture it and invest in its future. It's sometimes difficult for founders to separate how they feel about the business from how they feel about the people who work for them. This blurred line often means that founders see betrayals as intensely personal. The extent of the harm to future trust can be difficult for others to comprehend. While the CEO of a Fortune 500 company might be furious that an executive vice president leaves to work for the competition, he usually sees this betrayal more in business terms than in personal terms. But when a trusted FM or NFM leaves to work for the competition, it's traumatic—not just from a business standpoint but from a personal one too.

We have many FOB clients who have been devastated by betrayals both from FMs and NFMs. It happens when trust is given to people who say they share your values but act in unethical ways. While these betrayals hurt both pocketbook and pride, there is always a great deal of learning for everyone involved. There may also be legal recourse. Our family has had to deal with theft of our intellectual properties. For all of us it has been very personal. Here's how Amy recalls one of the situations.

> When a wannabe partner in Kolbe Corp betrayed our trust by stealing our intellectual property, we were all furious. That someone we had trusted—and trained in our programs—had ripped off our test and sold it to others was despicable. But when we discovered that he had been making up a score that gave people who used it wrong advice, Kathy felt a deep sense of grief.
>
> "He has not only abducted my child," she said. "He's raped her."

Ironically, betrayals of trust can often bring employees of an FOB closer together. As they communicate their thoughts and feelings about the betrayal, they close ranks. NFMs are usually as incensed as the FMs are. The betrayal hurts everyone involved, so they come together both to rant and to consider better ways of protecting the company.

Why is an FM's betrayal double jeopardy?

When the betrayal of the FOB comes from an FM, negativity often reverberates throughout the business and the family.

> Gertrude had to explain to her four grandchildren why she had to fire their father after he had falsified his travel expenses. Or did she? Could she pretend it didn't happen and sugarcoat his leaving (at least to them) as a need for him to "expand his horizons"?

> Burt and Sally had helped grow the company his dad founded (and of which he was still the majority owner). When they realized that his dad had been talking about selling it behind their backs, they wanted to walk away. Would they ever be an intact family again if their leaving the company while it was up for sale lowered its value? Was the damage to the family already done by his dad's actions? What about the financial security of Burt's mother, who knew nothing about any of it? Could any of this be resolved in a way that would salvage family relationships?

> It was stupid of Tiffany to share the secret formula for the FOB product with her girlfriends. "Yeah, but, I didn't mean to do any harm." Yeah, but . . . her friend gave it to a friend, who gave it to a friend, who put it online. . . . "There is no putting that genie back in the bottle," Tiffany's older brother, Slate, said. "Everyone knows it was a family member who literally robbed us of our intellectual property. That makes us all look stupid and irresponsible, on top of everything else."

Business consultants' advice for how to deal with these kinds of problems will not change the dynamic if they don't understand the importance of factoring in the entirely different approach you have to take with FMs.

A spouse who is betrayed financially cannot begin to solve the business problems without first dealing with the emotional abuse. There may be moments of intense feelings—even hatred; there may be temptations to overreact and deal a "You deserve it!" penalty that could jeopardize the business future. Strong emotions can lead to poor decisions.

Don't confuse making mistakes with unethical behaviors. If Tina makes the wrong calculations and the deal ends up costing too much, blame her cognitive math skills, not her integrity.

The choice you make to act or not to act is how your values play out as either ethical or unethical behaviors.

- "I felt it was the right thing to do" can take an employee off the hook for what might have looked like unethical behavior, but it doesn't make it okay not to have considered the cognitive facts.

- "I did what I was told to do" may be absolutely true, but following unethical orders is not a defense for committing a crime.

- When you don't contact a friend who was injured in an accident while a passenger in your car to see if she is okay because you fear a lawsuit, you show a lack of trust in the friendship.

How to repair broken trust

Even after trust is broken, it's possible to restore it. As ghastly as a situation may seem at the time, unconditional love can heal a lot of emotional wounds. What makes the damage doubly difficult also provides the motivation to find a way to make things better.

No one can cause greater harm to an FOB than an FM who violates a trust, but because this is family, you will probably do whatever you can to offer this person a chance for redemption. Leaders in this situation need to ask themselves, "How likely is this issue to come up again, and what do we want to have happen now?"

If some FMs aren't willing to work at rebuilding trust with the errant FM, it will require tough decisions. Here are two important considerations to discuss:

- Would trying to rehabilitate that FM cause a rift among other FMs?

- If so, are there greater problems within the family leadership group that need to be addressed?

Be careful if you decide to bargain for a truce. Those rarely last for very long. If you just look for peace at any price, the price will almost always be too high.

BEST PRACTICES FOR REBUILDING TRUST

Decide on an appropriate reparation or penalty for the specific harm that was done. This includes such actions as removing or adjusting titles; responsibilities; travel and other benefits; or bonuses, commissions, or other financial considerations.

Make certain that everyone who knows what happened is aware of the consequences. Communication is key.

Try to rebuild trust during a cooling-down period in which small degrees of responsibility are given back.

Get professional guidance, if necessary.

Help FMs who've blown it find opportunities to rebuild trust with NFMs. Don't admonish the NFMs, however, if they back away from the situation or give the person a hard time.

We tell NFMs to trust their instincts. If they don't believe they can rebuild trust with an FM boss, they should either seek reassignment to work with people they do trust or ask for a positive recommendation for employment elsewhere.

What if you're the FM who has betrayed the trust of other FMs? If you have done that, then honesty is the best policy. Be forthright, own up to mistakes or problems—and grovel, if you have to. Forget trying to save face or get favors.

If you screwed up, own up. If you don't do that, you will live and work in an environment rife with tension and suspicion. It can make you and your immediate wing of the family extremely uncomfortable at holidays and other family gatherings for the rest of your life. So just bite the bullet, confess, and apologize. Just do it!

Reality Checks: Questions to ask yourself

✓ To what degree are you trusting your own instincts?

✓ Does the organization allow everyone the freedom to act on their instinctive strengths?

✓ Is there a double standard in forgiving errors made by FMs more than forgiving NFMs?

✓ When appropriate, what process is used to repair trust that has been broken?

✓ How are situations handled when what is best for the company is not necessarily best for an individual FM?

CHAPTER 5

Boundaries That Build Better FOBs

Setting boundaries among FMs is as important to your FOB as putting a fence around a swimming pool. Without work-related boundaries, FMs can dive into the business, get in over their heads, and drown. Others may never choose to swim in a pool where that has happened.

Call them boundaries, limits, borders, guidelines, demarcations, thresholds, or thalwegs; what's essential is that you draw a line between what's acceptable and unacceptable in your FOB. Here's how:

- State them clearly.

- Note them often.

- Adhere to them, even when you wish they weren't there.

- Change them when they become too rigid.

We recommend using fuzzy logic in setting those boundaries. That means having simple *Do*s and *Don't*s guidelines, recognizing that there are some circumstances in which it is kinda the right approach and others where it will sorta work. Kinda like depending on airline schedules—yet planning for worst-case scenarios and being sure no one dives into the deep end.

The good news is that FOBs, even as they become giant corpora-tions, are not very likely to establish alienating, silo-type boundaries. They tend to give employees freedom for their creative efforts, allow flexibility in responsibilities, and don't get hung up on org charts. In fact, the org charts they design are often ignored.

They do this for the same reason they often have better benefits than non-FOBs do with a similar number of employees. Their leaders have to live with the boundaries they set.

Benefits of flexible boundaries—with cautionary tales

Relaxed boundaries of many FOBs become benefits for NFMs as well as FMs. Unless you love the rigidity imposed by more impersonal corporate structures, you may thrive in an FOB that is open to pro-viding options.

As with most good things, of course, these benefits can be taken too far—resulting in, "Oh NO!"

LESS HIERARCHICAL DECISION MAKING

"Oh NO! We all thought you were the one who would decide on the holiday vacation schedule."

BROAD-BASED EXPERIMENTATION WITH IDEAS AND EQUIPMENT

"Oh NO! You let the interns try out the gizzmograph and they messed up its gigoscope!"

AD HOC MENTORING

"Oh NO! I hear you gave Jeb the backstory on our problems

with the vendor. Unfortunately, Jeb is now a possible witness if we're ever sued over what happened."

INFORMAL EXPLORATIONS OF STRATEGIES

"Oh NO! We came up with great ideas in the brainstorming we did last month, but Lionel walked out the door and gave them to his new employer."

OFF-SITE MEETINGS MIXED WITH PERSONAL TIME

"Oh NO! Remember that terrific strategy we came up with at the BBQ? I don't. Seems no one wrote it down."

UNSCHEDULED OPTIONS FOR TELECOMMUTING OR REMOTE WORK

"Oh NO! Giving her the freedom to come and go made Deb gobs more productive, but investors are dropping by, and she can't get back in time to do her show and tell."

IMPROMPTU CELEBRATIONS

"Oh NO! When we realized we'd hit our target for the quarter, we turned lunch into a pizza party. Sorry we didn't do it when you could join us. We truly do appreciate your significant contributions."

INFORMAL RESETS OF WORKFLOW

"Oh NO! Glad it worked well when I took my people off task to help you with the conference, but no, I can't do that every time your team gets a work overload."

CASUAL TRAINING AND INCLUSION IN LEARNING OPPORTUNITIES

> "Oh NO! Terrance thinks you taught him everything he needs to know about our business, so he's going to go start his own business."

The most fundamental boundary is to keep business matters at the office and to keep family matters at home. We've seen many situations where FMs bring their personal issues into the workplace. That's not only awkward for other employees; it is unhealthy for the relationship and completely unproductive for the business.

> One wife manipulated her husband's schedule so he'd spend more time at home, but when he missed important meetings, their employees knew why it happened—and resented it.

Behaviors that don't belong in the workplace may seem obvious, but we could share hundreds of examples of inappropriate arguments and FMs poking their noses into other FMs' departments simply because they have not followed these basic guidelines.

The *Dos* and *Don't*s that make the biggest difference

While there are several *Dos* we want to share with you, we only have one *Don't*. Because we've seen it be a drop-dead issue, this *Don't* is a do-or-die necessity for FOBs.

DON'T BRING FM WORK RELATIONSHIPS HOME

If you learn nothing else from this book, we urge you to never cross this line.

If you are the boss at work, that does not give you the authority to dictate what you will name the dog.

You may be an expert in financial matters at work, but you don't get to decide how to spend the family budget.

Different views about product development are valid and valuable at work. Opinions about another FM's fiancé/holiday plans/haircut are not. Keep personal time personal. Only when a recreational activity involves customers, clients, or other employees should there be any discussion of the business appropriateness of how FMs use their time off.

Even if you are their boss at work, do not tell fellow FMs,

- "We need you to come back rested from your vacation, so don't do too much partying."

- "Here's some reading it would be good for you to do over the weekend."

- "I don't want you representing us until you lose weight."

- "The places you are going on dates are certainly not places where I'd like our clients to run into you."

- "You need to host the next office party at your house."

- "Stop spending so much time watching sports so you'll have more time to keep up with finance issues."

DO CONSIDER PRE-FOB CONTRACTS FOR SPOUSES

Pre-FOB contracts should be lots easier to draw up than prenup agreements are. Pre-FOB contracts, after all, would be agreements about how you would make money together, not how you would divide it up if you stop being together.

Yet, we actually know of no one who has created a pre-FOB except Kathy and Will. It was written on the back of an envelope. It's worked very nicely.

You are unlikely to get it notarized (they certainly didn't), but it's a good idea for spouses, and other FMs, to have a clear agreement of the ground rules before they start working together in an FOB.

Setting wise boundaries improves the odds of making it work.

The first issue that needs to be addressed between spouses is whether or not they have the right MOs to work directly with one another or if they need to work independently. Conative conflict is a leading cause of employee problems in any business. When it happens between FM spouses working together, it can harm productivity as well as relationships.

Husbands and wives usually have different roles in the family, which can impact the roles they automatically start off performing in an FOB. Far too often these roles follow the cultural sexism that has the husband serving as the strategist and the wife serving as the bookkeeper and office organizer. When those roles don't fit their MOs, trying to fill them can lead to personal and professional stress.

Don't fall for claims that men take more risks than women do. We have 40 years of research showing this is just not true (see the appendix).

Our recent research reinforces this.

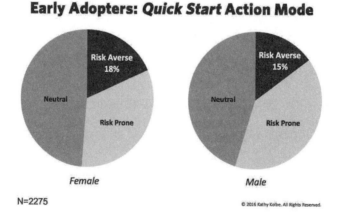

Early Adopters: *Quick Start* Action Mode

Female   Male

N=2275

© 2016 Kathy Kolbe. All Rights Reserved.

What is true is that some men take more risks than some women. And, some women take more risks than some men. The inborn drive to initiate risk ties to the Quick Start mode.

Quick Start Initiators seek out the type of risks that deal with uncertain outcomes. They are the explorers and innovators who experiment to see what will happen. That's the opposite of Quick Start CounterActors (aka risk managers), who try to reduce the probability of risk and who do not appreciate surprise parties.

In addition to these differences in types of conative risks, there are risks that have nothing to do with how people take action. They are emotional risks (usually tied to fears) and intellectual risks (usually dealing with unknowns).

Most of the so-called research on risk taking does not define these differences either in the way information is collected or the conclusions that are drawn. They interpret women's social behaviors, such as grabbing hold of a boyfriend in a scary movie, as signs of being risk averse. That, too, may change over time.

What hasn't changed over time is that the quantity and the quality of how human beings Initiate, ReAct to, and CounterAct risk is not determined by gender, age, or race. Both aspects of risk taking are determined by individuals' MOs.

In the general population, 20 percent of both males and females Initiate in each conative Action Mode—and 20 percent of both genders CounterAct in each Action Mode. So there are as many husbands who should be doing the books as wives, and as many wives who should be making the sales calls as husbands.

Since we know that there are equal percentages of males and females in each of the zones in all four Action Modes, we know that there are as many natural born female entrepreneurs as male entrepreneurs.

Every couple needs to figure out what works best for them. If that breaks stereotypes, so be it. Celebrate the freedom you give each other to be who you are.

If the husband is an Initiating Fact Finder, doing the strategizing will work out well. But if he Initiates in Quick Start, he should get out and sell. The same principle of targeting natural talents toward efforts that make good use of his MO should be utilized to determine the role for the wife.

> "Don't 'Honey' me," a wife snapped at her husband. "Everyone around us knows you're doing the work that you love to do, and I'm doing what you love to have me do."

Once she made clear what wasn't working for her, they figured out a way they both could have the freedom to contribute their conative strengths. She is a great bookkeeper, and 16 years later she's enjoying his calling her "Honey" at home and "Madame President" at work.

It's not unusual to have power struggles between spouses. They happen at home every time one tries to get the other to take out the garbage. When the issues become more significant at home for a couple that works together, boundaries need to be set to keep that stress from bleeding into the work environment.

Our Takes Two program (see the Selected Products and Services at the back of the book for more information) assists couples in reducing conflicts at home by increasing awareness of how conative needs play out in their personal relationship. The number-one way to prevent marital stress from damaging working relationships is to change the tone of communication at the office. In particular, each spouse needs to drop any sarcasm or snarkiness that indicates to others there is more to the discussion than business issues.

It's a lot easier to separate roles between couples when their conative MOs differ. The bigger challenge is dealing with spouses with similar strengths, who therefore should be doing similar tasks. That's a formula for getting in each other's way. Just look at these examples:

> **Fact Finder Initiating spouses** benefit from defining separate strategies for different aspects of the business (one sets priorities for operations, personnel, and finance; the other sets them

for development, sales, and marketing). They ought not to edit each other's writing.

Follow Thru Initiating spouses can prevent frustration by separating their areas of responsibility with clear boundaries. Those can be by geography, product lines, customer types, or time. They ought not to create competing filing systems.

Quick Start Initiating spouses can benefit from shared challenges, but they need to set boundaries so they don't try to one-up each other, or end up distracting from each other's efforts. They ought not to do presentations together.

Implementor Initiating spouses need space and time to work on their individual projects. They can work side by side, but they need their own personal workspace where they are able to manipulate their own sources of light, sound, and air. They ought not to use each other's tools.

DO ANTICIPATE SIBLING RIVALRIES

No one ever seems to completely outgrow sibling rivalries.

Even siblings who dearly love one another can have trouble working together because Dad used to praise one and not the other. Or, Mom gave the easy chores to "her favorite." No matter how much baby boomers learned about sharing and openness, or earlier generations discussed "quality time," siblings from every generation have lots of issues with each other.

Think about it. Do you know anyone, of any age (other than an only child), who doesn't tell stories about their conflicts with at least one sibling? Siblings know what buttons to push to get the reactions they want (recall the examples in chapter 4 in the discussion titled "The power of knowing FMs' instinct-based truths"). Regrettably, that behavior in a workplace setting can destroy relationships.

There is a false assumption that siblings know each other well enough to know how to work well together. Knowing a sister's hobbies does not tell you how she will handle a client meeting. Sometimes sibling rivalries are caused by natural conative conflicts, but often they are the result of false expectations based on a gender or age bias.

It's not unlike the boundaries for spouses; siblings are responsible to keep their personal baggage out of the workplace. "Staying in your lane" helps make this possible.

A case we know well

David and Amy, working together now as principles in Kolbe Corp (the business founded by Kathy) are, as we mentioned, stepbrother and stepsister—without all the baggage. That's not because Kathy was the perfect mother. It's because they met when both were in college and became part of a blended family. Therefore, any imbalances in tooth fairy payments were free of parental biases. Here's how Kathy describes their becoming coworking FMs.

> Amy preceded David in joining the business. Her successes as a senior trainer and regional manager in another business made both of us confident she could handle her assignments. She quickly established her best areas for making a contribution in training and sales.
>
> David grew up proofreading my publications, being a guinea pig for every assessment I created, and having to listen to my business calls. I held off recruiting him until after he had succeeded in jobs as a congressional aide and as an attorney.
>
> While they had become good friends and were supportive FMs, working together was a new situation for Amy and David. The immediate fit was their shared commitment to the mission of the company. Differing backgrounds made it easy to create the boundaries for their contributions. Their

unique paths were clearly defined, but the levels they would attain in the company were entirely up to them.

The first boundary I set with Amy was that her job would be short term. We agreed that after six months of experience at Kolbe Corp, Amy would probably be in a position to look for other options that would fit her husband's professional baseball schedule. But, after three weeks, it was clear to me that Amy's strengths in all three mental factors (cognitive, affective, and conative) were perfectly suited to what I needed in my business. The time boundary was removed, replaced by an agreement that Amy would stay in Kolbe Corp for as long as it challenged her creativity and could be flexible enough for the crazy schedule of a baseball wife—and soon-to-be new mother.

Amy's work from many other areas of the country, through pregnancies, and during child-rearing challenges helped pave the way for the highly flexible boundaries the company set for other employees.

When David joined the company, it was apparent that his background, skills, and interests were well suited to areas that were not part of my strengths or Amy's. From the get-go, he worked in the legal, financial, and technical aspects of the business. To the great benefit of Kolbe Corp and me, there has never been a problem keeping the role definition between Amy and David clear.

As important as it was to create boundaries, flexibility was needed when one or the other of them was out of the office because of vacations, births, or kids' health issues. Even before they assumed senior leadership roles, it was essential for each of them to know enough about the other's roles to personally fill in.

Boundaries continue to be important for all of us as the company grows and as the management team responds to Amy's and David's differing approaches—plus the ones I bring in from my enterprises that are now outside of Kolbe Corp.

What if Amy had aspired to the role of CEO? Both she and David knew they had equal opportunities for that. But the role does not suit her MO, so open discussions made their eventual shared ownership and titles play out in natural, logical ways.

Setting boundaries around separation of duties becomes even more important when any two FMs have significant differences in their conative approaches to problem solving. Conative conflicts, unlike affective "personality differences" or cognitive differences in opinions, are not helped by lectures or training. It's not about how much individuals like or respect one another.

Conative conflicts are real, they are everlasting, and they can lead to great frustrations. They can also be the source of wonderful collaborations if they are recognized and used as a means for separating tasks into the most viable ways for getting things done. Just as it has been for David and Amy, working independently toward common goals is often the best way to leverage your different strengths.

DO RECOGNIZE CONFLICTS BETWEEN FAMILY AND BUSINESS LOYALTY

It shouldn't happen, but it does.

Frank is the CEO of a construction company. The long-time CFO is his niece, Sara, whose husband is a company carpenter. During contract negotiations with the tradespeople, Sara took offense when Frank said they had to get a handle on escalating labor costs.

"She took the side of labor in front of the entire management team," he said. "She's supposed to be advocating for
our financial security, not her husband's paycheck."

Yes, but . . . can you blame her? Frank did because he paid her
to protect the company's financial position, and for him, Business is
Business. She did it because Family is Family, and she listened every
night to her husband rage about being underpaid and not appreciated
for his critical contributions. She knew where the profits were made
and what his contributions were.

Conflicts often exist between loyalty to an FOB on one side and
loyalty to a labor-minded spouse (and his or her family) on the other
side. Family issues usually override business issues. Rarely do the FMs
who have these conflicts stay in the business.

Knowing this, we advised Frank to listen carefully, trust his
instincts, and not put Sara in the awkward position of having to
choose between her spouse and the FOB. Frank had to work through
the impasse in a way that would save face for everyone and not cause
family dissension. In the end, he needed to be an understanding
uncle (even if he didn't feel that way) who gave her a reference for a
position in a different company—one that wouldn't have this conflict
of interest.

DO PROTECT ACCESS TO THE CORPORATE SECRETS

FOB leaders have business secrets that need to be shared with others.
These often involve complex situations related to finances, personnel,
or intellectual property that leaders need to discuss with trusted con-
fidants. It's not unusual for both FMs and NFMs to be among those
brought into such discussions.

We, and several of our clients, have experienced the agony of trust
given in such situations being broken. Therefore, we sadly say, better

to err on the side of paranoia about keeping business secrets. Don't suffer sleepless nights wondering why you let your child travel with the wrong friend.

Assets such as intellectual capital and commercial secrets are the mainstay of our FOBs. The same is true of many of the FOBs we counsel. Our employees need to understand that their futures with the business are as much at risk as are ours if competitors get hold of them. It would be like giving out the formula for Coke, or letting people make copies of the key to the castle.

Even then, only the most reliable employees—who have the most to lose if the secret formula got out—should have any control over access to the hiding places. Yes, plural places. Think fire, floods, tornadoes—and forgetfulness. There have to be alternatives, because calamities can wipe out secrets that are hard to remember.

DO SET SPACE AND EQUIPMENT BOUNDARIES

FMs have many fewer boundaries about sharing things than do other coworkers (even though some sisters fight over taking things out of each other's closets). It is easier for them to share a desk, a client, or the plans for a company party than it may be to do the same with NFMs.

When FMs share a strong sense of purpose and personal closeness, their reliance on one another and sharing of information may be viewed as favoritism by NFMs. For that reason, pay attention to the following policies and procedures regarding workspace for FMs:

- Make a policy to distribute FMs workspaces so they don't cluster together.

- Don't give them higher status locations than their jobs would normally merit.

- Give them the same type and quality of furniture as others in their type of jobs.

- Have them abide by the same guidelines and traditions regarding art and supplies as other employees.

- Don't give them power over the color of the walls or design of the office unless they are senior enough in the organization to merit that level of decision making.

DO AVOID UNNECESSARY BARRIERS BETWEEN FMS AND NFMS

It's wonderful when NFMs become like members of your extended family. Sometimes such relationships grow to the point of being able to trust an NFM more implicitly than you can an FM.

> Raul began his career in a software development company at the help desk. He was an excellent communicator who took a great interest in learning all he could about the business. All three siblings, who are the partners in the company, ended up wanting him in their departments; so, they wisely had him rotate among them for several months each, and found marketing was the best place for him. In the process of doing this, Raul became almost like a fourth sibling. They often worked late on problems together and would frequently go to sporting events together.
>
> While Raul grew to love the siblings, and they trusted him implicitly, he had an uncanny way of knowing the boundaries. When it came to family-only decisions, he would excuse himself.

It was not a matter of Raul "knowing his place" in the sense of being less important in any way. He exemplified how, even in personal situations, an NFM may be there to help as much as most of your FMs. Maybe even more so. The FMs in this case all think of Raul as "family," but he wouldn't think of assuming any ownership-level behaviors while at work.

> In the case of Brigitte, on the other hand, she never figured out appropriate boundaries while working with a family she adored. She was the executive assistant to the CEO of an FOB. Initially, he greatly appreciated all that she tried to do to help with his family situations. He had four FMs working in the business and a big extended family at home. She was excellent at integrating his personal and business schedules, purchasing gifts, and summarizing the needs of both the FMs and the NFMs in his life.
>
> Shockingly, her boss told us that Brigitte became far more of a liability than an asset.
>
> "She tried to insinuate herself into all my relationships," he said, "including coaching my daughter on how to get special favors for her department, and even telling a VP when I was too busy for him to ask for a meeting with me. She got so involved in FMs' personal lives that she had no objectivity about them as employees—and even got mad at me when I criticized some of her personal favorites among them for their obvious mistakes."
>
> Brigitte tried to become an advisor to both FM and NFM employees, based on a presumption of power she had as a family "insider." She was shocked to be reprimanded for doing this because she thought she was a part of the family, and that "family" meant you were "untouchable." When the CEO decided there was no way to turn the situation around, he let Brigitte go.

Be aware, too, of how you handle criticism of FMs in front of NFMs. While it's fine to have a heated discussion on a difference of opinion, it's not okay to criticize an FM openly. This is especially true when familiarity causes you to critique an FM in ways that you would never do with an NFM. While it's important to hold an FM accountable, have these types of conversations in private so it doesn't become awkward for all involved.

DO AVOID "US AND THEM" CLIQUES WITHIN THE FOB

Cliques rarely serve positive purposes, although sometimes, in very large companies, it is important to have smaller groups that have a sense of belonging for employees. Even then, it is best when those are made up of collaborators. Anyone within a company who tries to pit one group against another can interfere with the Synergy the company should be striving for.

It can be a serious matter for an FOB if a dissatisfied NFM tries to create an alliance among NFMs based on real or potential grudges. It rarely helps to have an FM try to ease the tension. This is where people like Raul play highly significant roles. FMs should regularly reach out to NFMs rather than sticking together in their own family clique.

Retain outside advisors who can facilitate discussions if tensions arise between any factions within an FOB. The owner and other FMs may be too emotionally involved in the situation to be able to set boundaries between personal/family issues and purely business considerations.

Remember, too, the importance of notifying other FMs of what and when you are sharing sensitive information—unless you are prepared to have an all-out fight if they find out about it later.

If the "odd couple" can live together by drawing a line down the middle of the room, you can work together with FMs and NFMs with these boundaries that won't interfere with sharing the work and the rewards.

Reality Checks: Questions to ask yourself

- ✓ Is there a clear delineation or definition of roles and responsibilities for each FM in the FOB?
- ✓ Have you ever let a family issue affect your business relationship with an FM?
- ✓ Are you trying to solve business problems at home?
- ✓ Are FMs' workspaces clustered together?
- ✓ Have there been situations in which something that should have stayed backstage occurred in front of the curtain?

CHAPTER 6

Telling It Like It Is—Or Not

Within FOBs, two languages are spoken: the common tongue of the company and the less common one the FMs have learned at home. Think about the latter form of communication and the ways it's different from the common one:

- FMs call each other by nicknames that may be unknown to other employees.

- FMs can communicate through expressions and gestures—familiar to them but not to others.

- FMs can discuss business problems in settings (home, private family dinners, vacations) that are exclusive to them.

- FMs know personal details about each other that can creep into business communication.

If you are an FM, you are probably unaware of how often your family's unique communication style bleeds into the business. Your lack of awareness can create an "us vs. them" mentality when you don't bring NFMs up to speed quickly enough.

Cracking the code

Nothing makes you less likely to succeed as an outsider in an FOB than not blending into its style of communicating. Yep, it's a double negative.

Whether it's verbal or nonverbal communication, the wise new-comer will pay attention to even subtle signals emitting from others and respond in kind.

> "You just never figured out how we do business," the FM told a department manager she was firing. "We literally have an open-door policy, but most of the time, you keep the door to your office closed.
>
> "Members of your department get together for potluck lunches. You eat in your office.
>
> "All the other managers weigh pros and cons together, putting in their two-cents' worth even when issues being discussed don't directly involve them. You never speak up unless we're discussing your department. Then, you pretty much tell us by your body language that you've already made a decision and you're not at all interested in what anyone else says.
>
> "Your lack of communicating in ways that make you blend into the team make it impossible for us to keep you on the team."

The manager was clueless, arrogant, or didn't care whether he kept his job when he ignored the obvious messages he was being given. He should have picked up on the signs that the FOB he was work-ing in clearly had an open-door policy, which made closing his door unacceptable.

There are lots of ways of dealing with a need for privacy (or whatever motivated his closing his door so often), but he never tried other options. His failure to discuss his needs was his downfall. The same was true of his apparent unwillingness to follow suit when other division managers put their problems on the table for open discussion.

FOB leaders, as well as leaders in any company, have a responsibility to clarify definable communication guidelines for newcomers. Closing the door when there is no need for confidentiality is an easy one to disclose.

Deciphering corporate jargon is another story. This can be quite challenging for NFMs in a family business. It's not easy to list all the idioms that FMs grew up using.

> "Don't contaminate the environment," Russell's coworker said to a newcomer.
>
> What the heck? She had no idea what she had done that stunk the place up.

It wasn't what she did. It was what she said. In that FOB, swearing was considered a pollution of the workplace.

FMs are wise to ask NFMs to create a list of some of the words and phrases they had to figure out when they came into the business. It can be great fun to share stories about when meanings became clear. The role of a company mentor for newbies could include sharing the list.

Your way is the right way

How information is communicated is purely conative. Being authentic requires communicating in your natural conative "voice." People described as having charisma communicate who they are more than they deal with what they know or want. Here's how it plays out:

Fact Finder Initiators use written words—and lots of them.

They include data and references and give complex examples. They send emails with lots of attachments.

Fact Finder CounterActors put words into brief bullet points. They summarize and clarify key points without much elaboration. They rarely read attachments to emails.

Follow Thru Initiators design charts and graphs. They organize information in spreadsheets, timelines, and checklists. They plan for white (or empty) space.

Follow Thru CounterActors take a highly flexible, scattershot approach that doesn't lock them into one format. They switch gears as needed. They create interesting clutter.

Quick Start Initiators say what they think, improvising or making it up as they go. They add colorful language, sounds, and looks to their messages. They call it like they see it.

Quick Start CounterActors start communications by sharing what is certain and try to decrease any discussion of uncertainty. This is their version of a good news/bad news approach.

Implementor Initiators demonstrate what they mean by using props and models. They communicate best when they can read body language. They show—they don't tell—you.

Implementor CounterActors will imagine solutions and share their abstract ideas. They don't need to see it to believe it.

Tricks for communicating naturally when your brother doesn't pay attention to your method of communicating always tie back to beauty (which is truth) being in the eyes of the beholder. The more you figure out how your parents will naturally react to your telling them another car hit you in your car, the more time and agony you will save yourself.

- **Don't** try to hide the details from your Initiating Fact Finder sibling.

- **Do** get right to the bottom line with your Initiating Quick Start parent.

- **Don't** scribble out messages to your Initiating Follow Thru grandparent.

- **Do** leave something you yourself made for your Initiating Implementor kid.

Keep these conative factors in mind when considering the following additional *Do*s and *Don't*s involving communications in FOBs.

The *Do*s and *Don't*s that make the biggest difference

The following *Do*s and *Don't*s, among all that are in this book, will cause people in any FOB the deepest regret should they decide to ignore them.

DON'T BRING UP BUSINESS ISSUES IN FAMILY SITUATIONS

This could save you from a whole lot of terrible, awful, very bad situations.

It's fine to talk about your goals, your philosophy, and your broad concerns with any and all FMs, but not at times such as birthday parties, other family gatherings, or holidays. It's appropriate to discuss issues involving trust, values, and development with those close to you, but discussing business deals over a birthday dinner can be off-putting.

> Rosa had spent the entire day running her FOB, then she stopped to pick up groceries on her way home. She got there with just enough time to put candles on a birthday cake for her youngest son, who was not yet working in the business.

Her other kids, José and Jamie, arrived directly from a sales meeting and joined the entire clan around the dining room table.

Before anyone had even filled a plate José announced, "Jamie lost a big sale for us today."

"No, it was you who blew it," Jamie said. "You interrupted me just as I was getting ready to ask for the order. You can never just shut up and let me do it my way!"

"You're always taking too long and bore the clients," José replied.

"You two stop it," Rosa shouted. "It's your brother's birthday and this is not the time for business arguments. If you keep carrying on like this, your brother will never want to work with us."

"You've got that right!" said the birthday boy. "When I blow out the candles, I'll wish that I never have to work in the family business. I don't want to have to bring my work home with me like they do."

DO ESTABLISH GUIDELINES FOR DISCUSSING BUSINESS ON PERSONAL TIME

One of the drawbacks for FMs who live and work together is losing their ability to discuss challenges at work with their favorite confidant at home. Agreeing to separate the need to vent about a problem from actually coming up with solutions together is a rule that can keep business and personal lives on a healthy path.

We are aware of situations in which violating this guideline has led to stress among FMs.

Amy was recently advising a woman who is part of her company's top leadership team. Her husband works one level below her in the organization. "It's been hard," she said, "because I talk about the company all the time. There are instances when he wants to come home and tell me about his challenges, but he seems to be holding back."

One day she told him that she knew he'd had a very bad day, and she asked why he wasn't telling her about it. "I'm not going to tell you," he said, "because I know you're not capable of just listening. You'll jump in and try to problem solve with me. I don't want to put you in that position—or add to the time we spend talking about work issues."

Agree ahead of time when and where you can discuss business issues that matter to you at home. Evaluate whether the communication boundaries you've established are working and be flexible, adjusting when necessary.

With a spouse, don't even think about bringing up business at a candle-lit dinner. However, it's not a bad idea to go to a "paper-napkin" restaurant where you can sit and talk through a company issue. Hopefully you wouldn't have a business discussion on a ride at the county fair, but you might while you're out for a walk. The key is to find a neutral environment and don't let it distract from a fun event. It is particularly inadvisable to get in a heated business discussion while one of you is driving.

With next generation FMs there's almost never a good time to talk about work outside the company because the adult reverts to a more dominant role. If it's absolutely essential, schedule it during a cup of coffee or at a casual place and not over a full meal at a restaurant in case someone needs an easy escape.

All bets are off if the discussion you have to have with a family member involves a disciplinary issue. But when in doubt, keep it in the workplace with a third person present.

Here are some communication guidelines that work well for Kathy:

When Will and I made a decision that we would not discuss business at home at night, we defined business as transactional matters, not questions about people or big picture ideas. We've been very good at keeping even those discussions to a minimum. Editing each other's writing is the only exception. Even then, if it starts to get into the details, we'll save our comments for the next workday.

When we first started bringing laptops home, we would be watching sports on TV or talking about current events while sending business-related emails to each other. It wasn't until an out-of-state son stayed with us for a few days and noticed what we were doing that we realized how technology had changed the game. Now we only send reminder texts to each other while sitting in the same room!

If you don't have a solid relationship and mature communication skills to guide these discussions about work issues, you probably can't function effectively together. If your personal relationship is fragile, being in business together will be a disaster.

DO ADDRESS FMS IN THE BUSINESS BY FIRST NAMES, NOT FAMILY TITLES OR NICKNAMES

Drop *Honey, Darling, Pops, Mom*, and *Junior*. Using first names with all employees generally works best, though it can take time to get used to it. Maintaining a business relationship at work calls less attention to your family relationships. When a son calls his mother Kathy, it makes it clear to both of them—and to others—that they are speaking as businesspeople, not as son and mother.

After a seminar with a high-level sales team, a participant asked his brother, "Why doesn't Dad allow us to discount the slow moving inventory so we can get rid of it?" Another sales rep nudged his coworker with his elbow and smirked, "Why don't you ask Daddy for yourself?"

The son was horrified when that happened, and he told us, "See what I have to put up with! When my numbers are good, the others think I got some special advantage, and when they aren't, they tell me that I don't have to worry— my dad will take care of me."

That was an easy one for us: "Call him Bruce at work, instead of Dad, and see what happens."

This may seem basic, but it sets the tone for all involved, including NFMs. This guideline should apply to all FMs, even the youngest FM intern. Never lie or conceal a family relationship in your business, but don't make it part of the introductions. Introduce by job titles, not family connections.

DO BE AWARE OF YOUR NONVERBAL COMMUNICATION

Make yourself conscious of the nonverbal signals you're sending to and receiving from FMs. These signals can vary, but they involve things like rolling your eyes or giving each other "the look." You may think people aren't watching, but they are.

Do you stand up when an FM leader walks into the room? Or only for other leaders? Are you demonstrating the level of respect that is appropriate for a given FM's role? Be careful that family familiarity doesn't cause you to respond in ways that might be interpreted as disrespect. You may sneer at an older sibling when you're sitting on the couch discussing politics, but if that sibling is your boss, a sneer isn't acceptable.

What about hugging: When is it too much? If you hug the FMs in the office, you should be hugging the NFMs too. What about clients?

Business is Business. You have to decide whether or not it's appropriate or acceptable in your office environment.

Here are some common examples of nonverbal communication:

- Pierre stares at you when he thinks you are wrong instead of saying it out loud.

- Clara twirls her hair when she doubts you are telling the truth.

- Mitch taps the table when you've gone on too long.

If you notice your FM using these or other gestures or looks, you should interpret what they mean to NFMs in the room. As familiar as you are with what the FM is suggesting by his look or gesture, it will escape most NFMs. Or, even worse, it will create discomfort or confusion. Your best response: Use humor to provide insights as to what your fellow FM is trying to "say." Don't be judgmental or sarcastic. Just clarify and lighten the mood with humor.

DO BE CLEAR ABOUT WHAT HAPPENS ON STAGE AND BACKSTAGE

If you were in a circus family, the differences between front stage and backstage would be obvious. Most FOBs begin as entrepreneurial companies, which are a lot like three-ring circuses. Everyone has to pitch in and support the starring act, then run to the next, and then the next wherever and whenever they're needed. One minute members of the troupe are juggling, and the next they are holding the horses' reins.

When FMs are on stage together—whether doing a seminar, running a restaurant, or consulting with clients—the audience is not only watching the results but also criticizing the process.

> Amy: After David, Kathy, and I did a session at our user conference, a few people commented, "You guys really look like you actually like each other!"
>
> Kathy: Yes. We actually do have great fun together. But that doesn't mean we don't critique each other backstage.

Backstage you can make caustic comments and not offend one another. But the audience doesn't know your inside jokes or how you know what the other FM meant. There are boundaries to both what you say and how you say it in front of an audience.

NFMs are part of the troupe and eventually they get used to your family lingo. They are with you backstage. You can be more casual around them. But the extra scrutiny that FMs get when the curtain opens should never be forgotten.

The key is to be genuine because phoniness shows through. At the same time, be on your best behavior when on stage together. Save snarky comments for later.

In the social media arena, information travels fast and widely. You may mention a sibling's embarrassment as an adolescent or a possible acquisition, and before you know it, everyone knows about it. Therefore, adhere to the following guidelines for sharing information online as well as off-line:

- **Don't** share personal stories about other FMs at the office without carefully considering the consequences.

- **Don't** discuss personal schedules with NFMs who don't need to know about off-hour activities.

- **Don't** break trust with other FMs by not disclosing important business information before they find out about it on social media.

- **Don't** put any family photos or stories online without considering how it could impact any FM's career or business/professional life.

- **Don't** put backstage FOB situations on the front stage through social media.

While these guidelines may seem obvious, consider the adage "Loose lips sink ships." People don't mean to disclose sensitive information, or don't consider the consequences of doing so until it's too late, as these examples demonstrate:

- The grandchild FM of an FOB founder asked for prayers for her ailing grandfather on Facebook. His employees and investors had been unaware of his dire situation.

- An FM shared family reunion pictures on social media showing the FOB leader drinking and having a good time—just as the leader was being considered as a keynote speaker for a conservative organization's conference.

- A proud father ruined his son's reputation among environmentally conscious clients by telling stories about their tree-clearing binge on their wooded property.

DO KNOW WHEN TO EMAIL, PICK UP THE PHONE, OR MEET FACE-TO-FACE

Recognize the best form of communication with both FMs and NFMs. With an FM, you may find yourself engaged in a personal conversation when a quick text message would suffice.

Rather than reflexively resorting to a sit-down with your sibling when you're having a major disagreement, it might be wiser not to storm into her office and instead send a well-considered email. Emails allow you time to think about what you're saying and how you say it. But be careful: They can also come across as more abrupt than intended.

Conversely, with an NFM you might be more likely to send an email when it's more appropriate to talk in person or on the phone. You may be better off bringing an NFM into your office and making an emotional appeal for more focused efforts rather than using an email that isn't particularly motivating.

Don't waste people's time. Be careful not to use team meetings when personal conversations will be more effective.

> The CEO of a multinational FOB told us that we were the first consultants who ever recommended they reduce the frequency of management meetings.
>
> "We're spread all over the globe, so we need teleconferences to stay informed," the CEO said. "Emails don't work. Reading what my brother writes doesn't tell me how truly upset he is about a new policy."
>
> Yes, but . . . staying in touch with his brother's feelings didn't require meetings with the entire management team.

Operating from a distance makes it difficult for FMs to keep both the personal and the professional relationships working smoothly. What used to be conveyed in informal settings now requires a scheduled one-on-one conversation, not more meetings for the whole team.

It may seem strange to set appointments to have a casual conversation with another FM, but distance often makes it necessary. Thank goodness videoconferencing has become so easy and accessible.

DO COMMUNICATE WITH TRANSPARENCY AND HONESTY, BUT BE REALISTIC

This is a crucial rule when it comes to values and trust, but obviously, you're not going to share everything with everyone. Be transparent about this issue, though; make sure NFMs understand that you may keep some aspects of business strategy to yourself.

Similarly, most FOBs are not going to share their financial strategies with NFMs—for instance, when you're fattening up the business so you can sell it. If you aren't transparent with FMs about this, however, things will get very difficult during Thanksgiving dinner.

Problems arise when FMs can't keep a secret or don't have an "edit button." To save them from themselves and protect the business, you can't always tell them everything. Sometimes it's a matter of need-to-know, and people don't need to know everything in every role. It's important to protect your time and role boundaries.

> Steve and Caroline, who are a CEO husband and CFO wife working together in an FOB, have established clear boundaries when dealing with employee issues. If one of their salespeople keeps selling things at the wrong price and needs to be disciplined, the wife must know because she is keeping track of the sales numbers. But the CFO doesn't need to spend her time and energy dealing with an employee who is gossiping and causing problems in the office. The CEO will delegate the appropriate executive to deal with those types of disciplinary measures.

DO COMMUNICATE DIRECTLY; DON'T USE OTHERS TO MANIPULATE FMS

Every FM has to stand firm on this rule. Consider these more specific *Don'ts*:

- **Don't** convey messages from anyone—an FM or an NFM—who is trying to get to your parent (who is the boss).

- **Don't** promise to present another employee's point of view to your sibling.

- **Don't** talk to your daughter about a team leader's concerns about her presentation.

- **Don't** let anyone persuade you to tell your spouse that someone thinks what he is doing is going to backfire.

When this rule gets broken, it can create a mess. No one likes to feel manipulated, and go-betweens foster indirect communication that usually backfires.

> Teresa collaborated closely with the daughter of the founder at a non-policy-setting level in the company. She believed that the founder was out of touch with the possibilities social media offers for reaching a broader audience.
>
> "Why don't you set your mother up on Facebook?" she suggested. "We could be sure she gets a lot of great connections, and she'll see what's happening out there."

Business is Business. Teresa can suggest to her manager some ideas for using social media, and the manager might present them to the founder or to whoever makes decisions at the right time, in the right setting. (Plus she should not, in this context, have referred to the founder as "your mother.")

Even small companies need a chain of command so that FMs are not asked to lobby for others' concerns and so those close to FMs don't take unfair advantage of that access.

Conversely, don't use an NFM to carry personal messages between FMs either.

> "Delia is pretty mad that you scheduled the retreat on your anniversary" is a message that no employee should be asked to deliver.

Nor should an NFM have to tell an FM, "Your brother says you owe him part of the commission because he actually closed the sale."

This kind of behavior is common in all businesses, but the possibility of it happening is even greater in FOBs because FMs are often unaware of their habits. Allowing these dangerous undercurrents to prevail damages personal relationships and drags the business down.

Actions speak volumes about your values

When customers yelled at Martha's help desk employees, she realized that one of her FOB's core values would be to protect all employees from verbal abuse. It happened in the early days of her company dealing with Internet transactions. Typically, it involved CounterActing Follow Thru callers impatiently blaming the poor people on the phone for their own frustrations with unfamiliar processes.

"Next time it happens," Martha told the staff, "put the person on hold and transfer the call to me." Doing that communicated a few important messages to her employees:

- She cared about how her employees were treated.

- She thought their jobs were important enough that she got personally involved.

- She understood the issues well enough to resolve the problems.

Her message to the customers was quite clear: The company owner is personally leading the business and will not let you intimidate her staff.

Communication is how values, trust, and every other factor in this book are integrated into the work environment. If at any time NFMs who come into an FOB cannot adjust to the family tone and content of communication, bid them farewell. Being a good employee is not just a matter of doing the job; it is a matter of being a part of a family-based effort. It's a deal breaker not to be able to (or to choose not to) adjust to the way people in the business communicate with one another.

By the way, we recommend using the same logic regarding communication with vendors and advisors. If your attorney can't write things in language your family understands, get a new attorney.

Reality Checks: Questions to ask yourself

- ✓ Are you consistent in using first names or appropriate titles with other FMs in the organization?
- ✓ Have you ever been uncomfortable when an FM shared family information at work?
- ✓ Do FMs limit the time they spend talking behind closed doors?
- ✓ Are there reasons why NFMs would feel left out of decision making?
- ✓ Are you aware of inappropriate use of nonverbal communication between FMs in meetings?

CHAPTER 7

Developing Living Assets

How do you prepare relatives for roles in an FOB? The answer for some of them: You don't. If relatives show no interest in being involved in the business, or do not have the right natural abilities to be able to contribute productively to it, find other ways to nurture their talents. *Different types of grapes are better in different varieties of wines.*

Helping FMs find their niche

Our data confirm that all human beings are truly equal—at least in one way. We all have an equal amount of conative ability. That means we all have good instincts, but not the *same* instincts.

Where we use our instincts is determined by our interests and learned skills. Just because Uncle Charlie uses his instincts to win at poker doesn't mean he couldn't use them to make good stock market decisions.

> Your sister Lulu trusts her instincts when she sings in front
> of people. If she were interested, she could be selling your

products rather than being in Nashville trying to sell herself as a country singer.

When an FM has the right instincts to help out the family business, but chooses not to get involved, it can cause hurt feelings.

"I built this ranch for you kids," a father said to his son. "It's been a fabulous place to raise you. Now that I need you to take over parts of it, how can you just walk away?" The simple truth was that the son didn't want to be a rancher.

Working in an FOB should never be mandatory. It should also never be the fallback option in an FM's job hunt. It needs to be a place that maximizes the use of the conative abilities of the FMs who want to be a part of the shared purposes.

We can't always predict who will be leaders in the FOB based on their initial time in the workplace. We can predict that the environments that discourage their creative energy when they are young won't become places they choose to work when they are adults.

Some youngsters may show interest in the FOB just because they like to work with Mom, Dad, and other FMs, or for a variety of other reasons (it's more interesting than school, it's fun to use the equipment, they love challenging tasks, etc.). Others may be thoroughly bored and find it a drag to have to participate in work-related activities. For them it may feel like a study hall, or a place where they have to be on good behavior and can't have any fun.

By the time they are teenagers, it is usually apparent whether a youngster has both the interest and the right conative strengths to develop into a future leader in a particular FOB. All their life experiences can help them channel their energies into situations that are more probable for career success. That's when it becomes critical that there not be false expectations that force them into the business.

Six ways to prevent problems with offspring joining your FOB

We wish we had known these guidelines three decades ago, when we first were asked to help FOB founders. We trusted our instincts in the ways we handled family situations, but we couldn't be sure that what was working for us would apply broadly. Our global reach in management consulting resulted in thousands of situations in which business owners took us aside and asked for personal advice relating to FMs they were hoping to bring into their business.

> "My kid never wants to hear about what I do, let alone ever do what I do. How did you get your kids involved in your business?" asked a Frenchman who founded a winery.

> "I can't stand my mother always telling me what I should and shouldn't be doing. What made it work for the two of you to work together?" asked the CEO of a multinational FOB.

It wasn't enough to share what has worked for us. We needed to field-test our methods across many types of companies, families, and founders. What we suggest here are ways we've seen FOBs successfully develop second- and now third-generation FMs. This is a heads-up for parents, grandparents, aunts, uncles, older siblings—and all who can help them prevent these problems:

- **Don't** push any relative into the family business if it doesn't fit his or her sense of purpose.

- **Don't** make immediate or extended family members feel guilty if they choose not to get involved.

- **Don't** rely on relatives to fill roles when their MOs don't fit.

- **Don't** question loyalty if relatives don't choose to work in your FOB.

- **Don't** give more personal praise or attention to relatives who join the business (especially someone who reports directly to you).

- **Don't** be less supportive of the careers of those who do not join the FOB.

As obvious as these rules may seem, they are being broken every day, especially by well-meaning leaders. The business may bring in big bucks, but the family may pay too big a price. The price the family pays is usually strained relationships and dissension among its members. It leads to sides being taken.

The rancher never forgave his son for not "helping him out," nor did he encourage the son to follow his own instincts into studying neuropsychology. One result of the estrangement was that the son did not return to his parents' home very often. Everyone else in the family thought the dad was acting selfishly and unreasonably. Until the grandkids pleaded for vacations where their father grew up, the rancher felt like no one was on his side.

Put freedom to be yourself above business needs

A business that knows the MOs of its employees can put all of them in the most appropriate roles. When parent-/grandparent-owners of FOBs know the MOs of young FMs, they can help them make wiser life decisions—and support them in finding the freedom to be themselves.

A father cofounded a machine tool company with his buddies and recommended his son for a role there. He and his son had worked on lots of projects together, so he felt confident saying his son had what it took to manage quality control issues.

Since the company uses the Kolbe RightFit process (see Selected Kolbe Products and Services) when hiring employees, the son completed the Kolbe A Index when he applied for the position. Much to his dad's surprise, the results showed that he was resistant to the hands-on building instincts needed for the role.

"But, son, you've always done a great job putting machinery together with me," the dad lamented. "Why didn't that ability show up on the Kolbe result?"

"You're confusing your ability to show me how you made it work, Dad, with my ability to be able to do it on my own," the son said.

Range of Success™
for
Quality Control Manager

Son	Profile of Ideal Candidate
Kolbe A™ Result	Range of Success™

Fact Finder	Follow Thru	Quick Start	Implementor	Fact Finder	Follow Thru	Quick Start	Implementor
7	5	4	2	4-6	6-8	1-3	6-9

Be aware of the difference between what you can do, or have learned to do, and what comes naturally. Spouses, like parents, bring FMs into the business based on false assumptions of conative abilities. Chefs sometimes think their offspring or spouses are great with food, but in reality, they just were good at following family recipes.

Make careers fit all three parts of the mind

Finding the right career is a matter of matching both your interests and your natural abilities with what needs to be done and how you need to be able to do those things. Some FOBs offer diverse work opportunities, and therefore they can accommodate many different types of MOs. Others are professional practices (such as law and accounting firms, magic shows, and auction firms), which are more narrowly focused. Trying to cram many offspring into these narrow work frames is unlikely to turn out well.

> Larry started his software development company a couple of decades ago. At times he had to work hard to keep up with the opportunities; at other times he had to work hard to pay the bills. His wife left him during one of the tough times, and they shared custody of a son and a daughter. When it was his turn to have the kids, Larry would bring them to the office. Daughter Marcia hung out among the staff, watching what people were doing and asking questions about their work. Son Tom chose to read books or play computer games.
>
> By the time they were teens, Marcia was an amazing programmer and a leader in the school's tech club. Her dad was paying her to do some critical tasks for him as the business was expanding. Tom, an excellent student and a pretty

good athlete, had become captain of the football team. He didn't have a lot of time to work, but when he did, Larry used his son's communication skills to help write proposals and marketing materials.

Larry saw a future for both of his kids in the business. He was especially pleased that Marcia would be able to fill the always-critical role of head of IT. But, it didn't turn out that way. Her technology skills, combined with her cona- tive instincts to be an entrepreneur, led her to start her own software development company. Larry's attempts to per- suade her to lead his team almost drove a wedge in their relationship.

"Dad, I love you. I respect what you've done to grow this business. But it is YOUR business. Not MY business," Mar- cia said. "I need to do my own thing. Please give me the freedom to do that."

"This business gave you the opportunity to learn most of what you know. It's paid the bills for your education. You owe it at least a few years of payback," Larry said.

The problems Marcia and her dad faced involved all three parts of the mind. Affectively, Marcia wanted to help her dad in the business. Cognitively, she was certainly capable of doing the job in the FOB. Conatively, that job was not well suited to her.

We suggested that Marcia complete the Apt Careers online program (see Selected Kolbe Products and Services at the back of the book) developed by Kathy. It includes a new type of conative assessment that identifies how an individual needs to be free to work. The algorithms in it are based on Kathy's brain research, especially studies relevant to job- related stress. Results of the assessment led to career recommendations for Marcia, including a 20 Best Careers report that indicates she has a natural conative drive to be entrepreneurial. Seeing the results helped her dad understand that helping her fulfill her purpose in life was more important than her filling a role in his company.

Marcia's Best Careers

apt careers

All of your 20 Best Careers have been chosen for you because they are least likely to cause you stress and most likely to lead to your success.

Entrepreneur

IT Mission Advocate

Innovation Strategist

Negotiator

Crisis Manager

It all made sense to Marcia when she saw the results. We understood this was a disappointment for her dad. Once he saw things from her point of view, he had many other questions. Had he cared about his business more than he cared about Marcia thriving in ways that suited her better? Did he not realize that she had earned everything she got from the business? Could they not continue to support one another on a personal level, without having her being involved in his business?

Conative consulting is different from affective therapy. We stuck with the action items in front of them rather than examining the way deep-seated feelings had influenced their behaviors. Larry decided to search for the right IT person for his company, which was his way of letting go of his expectations for Marcia being in the role. She helped him in the search and ended up introducing him to the person he hired.

Tom got an MBA and is now a vice president in his father's FOB, which didn't require that he become a programmer. Nevertheless, he's a strong leader in the company because of all the discussions he's had with his sister about how she manages her team of programmers.

It's hard to watch a Little League parent push his kid into playing the sport if the kid strikes out every time he is at bat. That's what it can feel like when a parent tries to force a son or daughter into a misfit role in an FOB.

It was logical for Larry to think that Marcia was prepared for the role he needed her to fill in his company. But her driving need, her ambition, is to fulfill her natural, entrepreneurial instincts. She has to have the freedom to be true to her nature, which is to be an innovative risk taker. Conceivably, she might have worked well with her dad in the start-up phase, but once his company was mature, she would have been ill suited for a management role.

Conative instincts determine *how* you need to work. Being free to do a job according to your innate conative pattern, or MO, is the key to success. Marcia's MO would not have made her as successful managing a department as it would in helping her start up a new enterprise. It was *not* an issue of her cognitive skills; they could be used in either role.

Our emotions drive us to do what we *want* to do. Marcia wanted to be in the tech world. She also wanted to make her father happy. Her emotions for self-survival (for freedom to be herself) were what determined her choice. That is usually the determining factor.

Just because you're born into a family with a business doesn't mean you were born with the natural aptitude to fill any or all of its roles.

Why your kids don't necessarily do things your way

Conative MOs are not genetic. Most kids do not have the same MO as their parents. This makes it tough, for example, to manage how they clean up their room—or not. A Follow Thru Initiator has a natural sense of order, putting everything back where it belongs at the end of the day. A kid who naturally CounterActs that process may get lots of extra cajoling, even punishment, for not doing what an Initiating Follow Thru parent thinks they should be doing. Unless this kind of hassling results in the kids developing a habit of putting things away (which is often not worth the effort), the tug of war will never end.

Some kids are natural born conative Initiating Implementors, endowed with a knack for building, being mechanical, making things grow, and other hands-on abilities. Going to an office and sitting in a cubicle would be a horrific day for such people in adulthood. You would likely see their energy level drop significantly because, instinctively, they get a sense of being caged in. And they would show little ambition to do much other than play computer games. Trying to make them fit into an internship that doesn't allow them to move around a lot could cause them to rebel.

An Initiating Fact Finder needs to become an expert. People with MOs like this are great at fact-checking, but they can get so involved, and go into such depth, that they miss deadlines. When you understand what drives their actions, you can help them strive for an 80 percent solution (or whatever works for the situation). Otherwise, they could be labeled a "perfectionist," which is a common concern about a Fact Finder who has not learned how to manage the degree of appropriate detail.

Larry understood that Tom is an Initiating Fact Finder, and this understanding helped him see why his son needed to get the MBA (which Larry had thought was a waste of money previously). It also explained why Tom read so much when it wasn't required, and why he could describe the benefits of some of their company's products better than Larry usually did.

Sacrifices can lead to resentment

In families where the parents were immersed in running an FOB, we often see an added element: grudges. Some of their children have felt that they didn't get the time and energy from their parents that they deserved because their parent(s) were so tied up in the business.

Their parents missed birthday parties, had to cut vacations short, or came late to school activities. If these kids join the family business as adults, they may harbor resentment toward it—and their parents.

> "My father always said that his kids came first, but it didn't feel that way," said a second-generation FOB member. "If I complained about his missing my ball games, I got the lecture about the business paying for the food on the table and the roof over our heads."

For many offspring of FOB leaders, the company can feel like the favorite child. These are just a few of the comments we've heard from them:

- "Mom would spend money on new technology, but I slept on a very old mattress."

- "My father and mother took their staff on a fancy retreat. I stayed home with a babysitter."

- "The business was supposed to pay for my education, but because of it my parents didn't have the time or money to take me places where I would have learned about the rest of the world."

- "It was never a question of whether I wanted to be involved in the business. As a kid I felt like an indentured servant."

These are also among the reasons some FMs give for not being committed to an FOB. It is understandable that kids can grow up feeling angry about "the sacrifices we all had to make" for the business.

The *Do*s and *Don't*s that make the biggest difference

Business is Business, and you certainly never want to do anything to harm it. But Family is Family, and you want to do everything you can to help family members succeed in life. We offer these guidelines as a way to help relatives become productive FMs to the greatest extent possible, without giving you cause to regret doing it.

DON'T GIVE A JOB TO FMS JUST BECAUSE THEY NEED WORK

If your kids or other relatives choose to come into your business, it must be a win–win: they want it and the business needs them. Don't let them join the business just because they have no other alternative.

Once you've decided to bring FMs into the business, create jobs that work for their MOs as well as their experience. Don't try to squeeze a square peg into a round hole. Instead, think about the types of roles that might suit them and also suit the business.

DO BE SURE YOU HAVE REALISTIC EXPECTATIONS

Greta, a senior partner in the law firm founded by her father and her uncle, remembers their law office being a very quiet and scary place to visit as a little kid. Until she was a teenager, she never went beyond the reception area, where she and her mom would wait for her dad. From there she could see into the glass-walled conference room where people in suits sat around a large table on chairs bigger than seemed necessary. Big, imposing chairs.

When her summer internship at the firm started, Greta was fearful of speaking too loudly, having her shoes squeak, or sneezing in an unladylike way. She rarely heard laughter there and figured that moving too quickly would disturb the people deeply immersed in computer screens or serious conversations. She couldn't understand why her fun-loving dad would want to be there for so many hours every week.

A young attorney was assigned to show Greta the ropes when she began the internship. The way he explained the work and the purpose behind it made it interesting to her Follow Thru/Fact Finder mind. She didn't just make copies of documents; she got to look through them and see how they related to a case her dad was taking to court. Helping to organize the paperwork for a trial was thrilling. Months later, she was allowed to skip school for a day to watch the case play out in the courtroom. That day she knew she was hooked. She, too, wanted to work in the family business.

Greta's parents believed that she might have a knack for the legal field, even though she believed that she would not enjoy working in such a formal, stuffy place. They were wise not to have her work there until she was old enough to act appropriately and listen carefully. The fact was that she had both the right MO and the intellectual capacity to tackle the internship, but timing was also critical.

Parents who hope their offspring will carry on the FOB need to cultivate their interest with timing and maturity in mind—and without making their hopes the highest priority. If Greta had not been intellectually capable of succeeding in law school, or had not had the conative instincts to excel in law, trying to mold her into becoming an attorney would have been a betrayal of her trust.

Once she understood the impact their work had in the lives of their clients, Greta knew this was work she wanted to do. It helped that her dad had often talked about the joy he found in helping people obtain justice. Her experience as an intern motivated her to become an attorney, and she did end up practicing in the family firm.

DO AVOID FEEDING FEELINGS OF ENTITLEMENT

Entitlement has always been an underlying problem in FOBs. Being an FM doesn't entitle adult children to walk in the door of the business as decision makers. Similarly, if these FMs accomplish something, they shouldn't expect special rewards. It was a long time before Greta became a partner in the family law firm. She had to earn it.

This is not an easy concept for kids who have been in an environment in which they got medals simply for showing up. If they are paid to work—or are unpaid interns—they are being fairly compensated in trade for the work they do. Only when they achieve extraordinary goals should they get special praise.

Next-generation FMs need to understand the importance of following the company policy and procedures, including dress code, working hours, and use of equipment. The actions of adult FMs should reinforce company guidelines regarding use of technology, including assumptions (often mistaken) about making copies of school papers, using company computers to get on social media, and personal use of things like art supplies.

It's great for offspring to see how hard their moms and dads work for each dollar the company collects, how important it is to keep expenses down, and how wisely time has to be used. These are not only important lessons for future leaders in the business; they can also help the next generation empathize with their parents when they come home tired!

DO REQUIRE FMS TO GAIN EXPERIENCE IN OTHER ENDEAVORS BEFORE JOINING AN FOB

There should not be many exceptions to this rule. You can set the stage, though. It's fine to say, "Someday I want you to work in the business." But you need to clarify that until the next-generation FMs prove themselves somewhere else they cannot expect a job in the family business—even when it's apparent they have the right MOs for specific roles.

Founders of FOBs often put their kids and nieces and nephews in the business without their having succeeded at something else. Second-generation FMs who know they'll go into the family business are often more social in school than committed to gaining the education that will prepare them for productive work. Taking for granted that a job awaits them upon graduation can limit their level of diligence in learning a profession, skill, or trade.

If relatives have just failed at a job outside the FOB, they need to go somewhere else and prove their ability to succeed. Never bring someone into the business who has a history only of failing at a string of various jobs.

Whether it's a child of the founder or a distant second cousin, these FMs must be able to walk in the door of the FOB adding value because of acquired knowledge, confidence, and respect. Without making sure they possess this value-adding ability, you are setting them up for negative reactions from other NFM employees who may have good reasons for believing that the FMs have not earned the opportunities they are being given as a "right of birth." It will make it much more difficult for them to integrate well with your other employees.

DO MATCH MENTORS BY MOS

Teachers can explain why things work the way they do. Parents can help you gain confidence in doing things your own way. Mentors can share tricks that have worked for them and are likely to work for you—but only if they share your natural ways of acting, reacting, and interacting.

When a mentor's mind works the same way your mind works, he or she can save you from many perils and guide you through many mazes. Here's how Kathy and Amy's mentoring relationship unfolded.

> Amy: Business courses I took in college taught me skills that have been extremely useful. Being a young ballerina taught me things that have helped me as a presenter. But no professor or ballet instructor ever gave me the kind of tips that dealt with how I could be myself in the ways I made decisions. That came from Kathy, who has an MO similar to mine.
>
> Kathy: Mentoring Amy was a natural fit, even though, by stereotype, I was the stepmother with whom she would likely have conflicts. In fact, I have far more natural conative conflicts with my son David. Much as I dearly love him, his insistence that I give his 8 in Fact Finder a great deal more specificity drives my 2 in Fact Finder nuts.
>
> "Really, David, you still aren't convinced?" I can hear myself saying. "What more can I tell you? My instincts

say, 'Do it!'" That's certainly not much help in his decision-making process. I could teach him values and role model perseverance, but I am a lousy mentor for him."

Kolbe developed a diagnostic report, the "Comparisons: A to A," that can identify potential conative conflicts like these and help any two people work together better, whether they are FMs or not. Here's what the reports show about the comparison between Kathy and Amy versus between Kathy and David.

Comparisons: A to A report
Kathy and Amy

How you gather and share information.	low
How you organize.	low
How you deal with risk and uncertainty.	low
How you handle space tangibles.	low

Comparisons: A to A report
Kathy and David

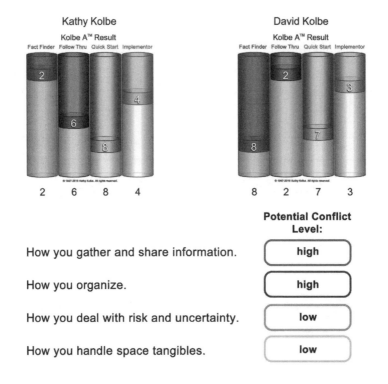

How you gather and share information.	Potential Conflict Level:
How you gather and share information.	high
How you organize.	high
How you deal with risk and uncertainty.	low
How you handle space tangibles.	low

Parents universally relate more easily to the child with the MO most like theirs. That has nothing to do with how close they are to each child. It's because they solve problems in similar ways. When their strengths are significantly different, it often requires going outside the immediate family to find ideal mentors for FMs. Sometimes it means going outside the FOB. The worst thing you can do is to assume that because you love someone you are the best person to mentor him or her.

Here's something else you need to consider: Who should directly manage an FM? When next-generation FMs join an FOB, it is *always* best for them to be managed by people with whom they have only a business relationship. In small businesses that's impossible. It is wise, nevertheless, to be sure that the chain of command is not broken by having a parent, who may be the CEO, manage the son, who comes in at an entry level. Even if there is only one level in between, it should be used to keep a parent from also being the direct manager.

DO GIVE FMS THE BENEFIT OF LEARNING FROM YOUR MISTAKES

We've rarely seen leaders in non-FOB businesses openly share their failures as part of the training of new employees. They don't write business books in which they honestly disclose their faults. Yet, we've noted that one of the benefits of having FOB founders as active members in the business is their ability to share stories of the backstage goofs in the formative years of the company.

It takes a very self-confident FM to talk about his or her biggest failures. It requires a lack of arrogance and an ego-free desire to help other FMs realize that mistakes happen, and they can survive in spite of them.

Mistakes we hear FMs share most often concern misjudgment of the character of partners, vendors, or employees. It's almost always about people problems. Being able to share this type of information freely is one of the great advantages of working in an FOB.

DON'T PROTECT FMS FROM FAILURE

"Helicopter," or hovering, FOB founders can do far more harm than good in the work environment. Overprotecting rarely happens to NFMs, but "safe decision making" is a plague among many FMs and their FM mentors.

Some FMs try to protect other FMs in the workplace. Maybe it's the family honor they worry about—a fear that the mistakes of one FM will reflect on all of them. Maybe the FM is aware of a special need, illness, or circumstance that is interfering with job performance.

None of these protective reactions benefit the FM, however. It is through our mistakes that we learn important lessons. It is through our ability to fix them that we gain self-efficacy—and build trust. To deny anyone the opportunity to figure out solutions would actually be creating a handicap for that person.

One of the greatest favors you can do for all your employees is to give them opportunities to fail. Let's listen as Kathy and Amy describe their firsthand experience of one such opportune moment.

> Kathy: A perfect such opportunity presented itself several years ago when I started coughing while doing a seminar for about 150 leaders in education. I wasn't faking it; I needed to pause to take a drink and settle my throat.
>
> Amy: I remember that well. I was there to learn how you present differently in education vs. business situations. I was figuring out how to use some new content too. I brought you a glass of water and expected you to take a break. Instead, you took the glass and handed me the microphone.
>
> Kathy: I certainly could have just said, "Let's take a break." Instead, I decided to use the situation to give you a chance to take over for me with not a moment's notice.
>
> Amy: I just grabbed the mic and completed the thought you had left in mid-sentence. I had to make some assumptions about where you wanted me to take the group from there. Although you were clearly able to return to lead the seminar, you didn't. You sat on the sidelines and let me finish the entire section on which you had been training.
>
> Kathy: I made a decision on the spot that put you in a high-stakes situation, and you proved you could handle it. Once I saw how quickly you got into your zone, I wasn't about to take you out of it. From then on, every time I can, I copresent with you.

What would have happened if Amy had fallen flat on her face? Kathy would have given the group a 10-minute break, chugged a Diet Coke, and picked back up where she left off. Later, Kathy and Amy would have laughed about the different ways the people in the room had reacted, and at the very least, it would have been a teachable moment.

The stakes have to be pretty high in order to truly gain confidence. If we don't use opportunities that come along, or purposely create them, no one—FM or NFM—will ever be able to achieve their full potential.

DON'T PUT AN FM ON A PEDESTAL

Some FM relationships give FOBs a bad name. It happens when a founder or leader brings in a relative who they believe could never make a mistake or be at fault for any problem. It's "Daddy's Little Girl," or the wife who is his "Sweetie Pie," the brother who is "Captain Marvel," or perhaps—worst of all—the relative who just graduated from Harvard.

No one in their right mind wants to manage that FM. Even vendors and clients figure out that this is not the person they want to handle their account.

> The founder of an FOB told all managers that because they were going through tough times, they had to decrease their department payrolls by 15 percent. And, he made it clear to his CFO that his nephew in that department could not be laid off. That meant that the CFO would have to lay off a more qualified person with longer tenure. She laid out the situation for the CEO, who said he was sorry, but that was the way it had to be.

The CFO declined to follow this direction, explaining that the order to do so made her lose respect for the owner and that she would lose her team's respect if she followed it. She then submitted her resignation.

The founder had every right to retain an FM during downsizing. Assuming that the person in this case had been productive—just not as productive as others—the CFO had a right to present the nephew's name as the person to be laid off. A possible solution would have been to tell the CFO she needed to make a lesser percentage cut in her payroll in order to keep the nephew, but that she still needed to reduce the overhead by perhaps 5 percent.

DON'T USE NFMS AS "BABYSITTERS"

Excellent NFMs walk a fine line between doing the job they were hired to do for the business and doing what they believe they should do to create and maintain a positive relationship with FMs. Here's a case where a founder took unfair advantage of the NFM's effort to be loyal.

An NFM sales manager working toward quarterly goals was asked by the company founder to involve an FM in the sales training, including tagging along with the sales manager on some calls. On the first call, the potential customer asked the relative (a brother) how he was related to the biz founder who had the same last name. The brother launched into a description of how he had been there when the CEO had developed the products the sales guy was about to demonstrate.

As described to us by the sales manager, everything

went downhill from there. The brother was not current on the details of the latest version of the product and got into a tangled mess when he grabbed hold of it. Then he did a lame job of explaining the pricing structure when trying to add his two cents about the value proposition.

"It was awful," the sales manager said. "He had the right name and relationship, but none of the right moves. How could I correct a guy with his family credentials without looking bad? It was one of those times I knew I was losing a sale but had no power to turn the situation around."

It breeds resentment to ask NFMs to share their expertise to help FMs skip some rungs while moving up the company ladder.

Training, educating, or shoring up the efforts of an FM should never be an unspoken responsibility of either an NFM or another FM. As tough as it is for some leaders to admit there is a need for special assistance with some members of their family, being honest about it is essential. Therefore, frame the NFM's responsibility in a way that makes it clear the task isn't babysitting but training; that the NFM will receive credit by carrying out this task rather than feel like he's being used as a stepping-stone for the family's favorite son.

"I know you are carrying a full load and are on tight deadlines," you might say to the manager who needs to assist your FM. "And I will factor that into your annual evaluation because I'm adding another task to your list. I need you to help Jerry overcome his fear of using the equipment. I realize it will take your time, but I believe you are the best person to help him become a fully productive member of the team. It would mean a lot to me if you would take on this assignment. Can I count on you to give it a try?"

DON'T ACT ON GENDER BIASES OR
BELIEVE BIRTH ORDER MYTHS

Our research shows that there are no gender differences among conative MOs. Girls are just as likely as boys to have a knack for math. Males are just as likely as females to be klutzes using tools. (For more information on this research, see the appendix.)

All too often, parents place FMs in roles in their FOBs based on gender stereotypes. It's bad enough when society limits your opportunities; it plays out even more sadly when your own family misreads the ways in which you need to be able to contribute.

The same is true when bogus birth order beliefs drive parental guidance as well as underlie the career paths they offer their offspring. Here's how Kathy now views what seemed "the way it is" when she was growing up.

> It was natural at the time for Dad not to consider I would become a leader in the Wonderlic business. I was, after all, a girl. There was a brother, as well as a brother-in-law, to partner in leading it through our generation. Men ruled the business world at that time.
>
> Now I realize that there was another reason Dad never considered me in such a role. While he spent copious hours teaching me how to develop mental assessments and discussed his philosophy of leadership with me, as the "baby of the family" with three older siblings, he clearly assumed that if I ever worked in the FOB, it would be as a test developer and researcher.
>
> Some writers have claimed that there is something about being the youngest that makes people not assume leadership roles. In FOBs, at least, I believe it is because it is difficult for FMs to see the baby (whose diapers they may

> have changed and baby talk they recall) as capable of being the boss of them.
>
> Dad, upon learning I had started my own business, warned his baby, "Kathy, find someone who can be the bad guy so you don't come across as a tough cookie."

Times have changed, with women now founding more businesses than men do. Nonetheless, the myths about abilities by birth order still hang on:

- Conative research proves the youngest in the family is just as likely to have the conative characteristics of corporate business leaders as the eldest. Yet, they continue to be less likely to be nurtured for those roles by their parents.

- Conative research also proves that "the middle child" has no greater probability of being accommodating in nature than any other child. Yet, their parents cause them to "see themselves" as more accommodating.

Every false statement about birth order determining conative type behaviors hangs on for the same reasons that false gender assumptions get repeated. They are self-fulfilling prophecies. They have been repeated out of ignorance of conative truths, to the detriment of millions of individuals—particularly in FOBs. Why more so in FOBs? Because, at least among those who have lived with you and who love you, there ought to be greater nurturing and more opportunities to be who you are.

DO USE THE SAME OBJECTIVE CRITERIA WITH FMS AND NFMS FOR SELECTION

FMs are almost never hired through the same process used to hire other employees. Sometimes, even though they lack the experience and expertise required of other employees, they are hired because of nepotism. Sometimes they are qualified for a position, though they may not be as qualified as other candidates; in such cases, they're hired because the founder "rationalizes" why they should be given jobs. Sometimes, even after they're hired, many FMs are placed in roles that may seem appropriate, given their accomplishments outside the business, but even though those accomplishments may be real enough, they don't translate to their business roles within the FOB:

- A successful novelist spouse may not be your best PR person.

- The head of the household may not be the right person to found a business or become the CEO.

- Just because a niece is great at putting on parties doesn't make her the right choice for event planning.

- An uncle may have made some great deals buying real estate, but should he be the sales manager?

Following the Kolbe RightFit Hiring System (see the Selected Kolbe Products and Services at the back of the book for a fuller description) ensures that you're using objective criteria when deciding if a potential FM is a fit for a particular role. Creating a profile of an ideal candidate includes the following:

- Defining strengths-based job requirements
- Analyzing the instinctive strengths of high performers
- Considering the problem-solving needs of the supervisor

Our data show that even married people who have been trained to interpret instinctive abilities are wrong over 70 percent of the time when guessing the conative strengths of their spouses. "But I know my wife so well," one man said. "She has always kept our family budget in good order. I was sure she had the Follow Thru conative ability to do that for the business."

Leaders in FOBs often presume that FMs will work well together because they know each other's strengths and foibles, share values, and can be trusted. If FMs do not have the right mix of differing conative abilities, however, they will make lousy team members. Without the natural Synergy it takes for FMs to benefit from working interactively, the attempt to do it can cause significant problems.

> "Donna may be the perfect wife and sister, but that doesn't make her an ideal new member of the development team," commented one FM.
>
> "What's Donna doing here?" asked another team member. "Maybe they thought she would keep us in line, or on budget. But all she's doing is slowing us down by trying to do more research—when we've already got plenty of people to do that."

It's bad enough that her MO adds a redundant ability. It's worse when Donna's selection creates morale problems because she seems to have been hired for reasons that have little to do with her abilities.

Balancing empathy for an FM with your commitment to the FOB

Empathy for and commitment to another FM can put an FM at odds with the best interests of the company.

The following are examples of gut-wrenching situations/challenges that affect the future of FMs and FOBs in ways that may not be mutually beneficial:

- Developing more than one of your offspring as potential leaders in the business and then having to choose which of them will be your successor.

- Fearing that you'll pigeonhole an FM by placing him or her in a job that is perfect right now, but you know there's not much advancement opportunity there.

- Bringing in someone who will be a supervisor above your spouse.

- Changing the role of an FM who is injured and whose loss of abilities (cognitive or physical) make it impossible for him or her to meet the demands of the job.

- Deciding how much time to invest in continuing to develop an FM who also has aspirations of running for political office.

All these issues deal with the return on investment (ROI) in FMs. And, although every situation is different, when we've seen remorse in these situations, it usually ties back to either poor communications or lack of empathy.

It is difficult to avoid *overthinking* your decisions about investing in FMs because those decisions are difficult to make. Likewise, avoid *underthinking* your decisions (snap decisions are dangerous territory) because you don't want to have to decide.

Reality Checks: Questions to ask yourself

✓ Have family stereotypes led to false expectations of your FMs' workplace abilities?

✓ Does your FOB provide equal opportunities for both FMs and NFMs to learn from failure?

✓ Have you ever recommended that an FM work for your FOB, primarily to help the person who may be struggling in his or her personal or professional life?

✓ Do you have any birth order or gender biases regarding the roles for FMs in the business?

✓ Does your FOB use the same objective criteria in the selection process for FMs and NFMs?

CHAPTER 8

Inciting Next-Gen Ambition

Too many FOB leaders put more energy into passing on wealth without passing on the secret sauce—the ingredients of creative problem solving—that creates wealth. Just as Olympic athletes, presidents, great teachers, and outstanding carpenters achieve through perseverance, so do top-quality business leaders. Whether you are a parent, an aunt, an uncle, a grandparent, or an NFM manager in an FOB, a significant part of your job should be developing a high level of ambition in the next generation.

Parents are forever looking for what's going to make their kids look good instead of what makes their kids work hard.

Developing youngsters' perseverance and resilience is a big job. Our culture hasn't been doing a very good job of it. Telling them they've done a "good job" when they made safe choices and didn't strive to do their best does not develop their potential.

To satisfy your own ambition, you have made tough choices. Would your kids, grandkids, nieces, and nephews be able to do the same?

Empowering the next generation to reach its potential

In physics, the definition of work is that it creates movement. Something has to happen. Thinking about something doesn't mean you worked at it. Next-generation workers need to realize that they need to *get conative* and put forth effort in order to achieve results. When one type of effort doesn't work, they have to learn to try another. This ambitious approach helps build the mental muscles needed to persevere.

People who show perseverance and resilience become heroes, and they should be universal role models. These attributes are essential for all successful human beings and should be tested frequently in FOBs. You're not just working for your own income and sense of purpose; you are responsible for providing financial security for other people, whether FMs or NFMs. You have to create a positive environment, with positive cash flow and positive prospects for the future.

We encourage you to enroll youth in a sport, an art project, a science club, music lessons, or perhaps chess if those activities would help them learn what it takes to try to work at something that isn't easy for them.

If kids have been in a position where they've worked against their grain and found it painful, they can understand the stress it causes. It will help them become empathetic with people who struggle to do what they do well.

Sowing the seeds of success

We've seen FOBs survive economic losses, fires, tornadoes, threats, and deaths. We have never seen an FOB survive heirs who lack ambition. Instilling respect for *doing the work* takes extra work on your part. It's always easier to do it yourself. But remember the saying about teaching a person to fish being more important than giving him a fish.

You can seed ambition from an early age and through the early teens. After that, you have to do a lot of weed pulling to get your offspring on the right path.

You incite ambition in your sons and daughters when you do any of these:

- Make a baby stretch and crawl for a toy.
- Insist schoolkids be responsible for earning their allowance.
- Point out role models for overcoming obstacles.
- Challenge them to strive for lofty goals.

Giving kids too many opportunities without having to work to earn them won't provoke ambition. If you don't encourage them to self-provoke, you are robbing them of part of their inheritance. The next generation needs to see you at work. Kids need to share the realities of how hard you work and the rewards you find from it.

An heir may say, "I don't want to have to work as hard as I've seen you work." He may not realize that when you are working according to your conative strengths it leads to the joy of accomplishment. Youngsters need to understand that the right kind of work brings a great feeling of accomplishment and that when they see you struggling against your conative grain, they are witnessing something that you and they should try to avoid.

Youngsters witnessing parents in conative stress because of having to work against their conative grain deserve an explanation. It may be just a situational stress that the parent has to get through in order to get a job done.

Youngsters often see hard work as highly undesirable. Part of maturity is knowing that being free to work hard doing something you chose to do is a blessing. Observing how hard work leads to achieving meaningful goals spawns ambition.

It's important for future FMs to understand the trade-offs that are involved when juggling work and family life. When it involves family sacrifices in order to achieve FOB goals, young family members benefit from being a part of the discussion, and whenever possible, their voices should be heard in the process of decision making.

"Dad, if the company moves into new offices, will there still be money for our vacation?"

"Son, I hope so, because we all want to go on the vacation. But the truth is, we need more space in order to meet our business goals. Reaching those goals could mean being able to go to an out-of-state university. Do you think that's worth giving up a vacation for? I consider it a part of our investing in your future."

That's a lot for a high school kid to absorb. Yet it's so much better to discuss the circumstances openly, let him express his thoughts, ask questions, and gain an understanding of the truths, and the consequences, of economic realities.

Kids we've seen participate in such seemingly conflicting family vs. business discussions receive lessons in creative problem solving, values, communication, economics, pride vs. humility, and empathy. Adults who fear such discussions will cause kids to worry and give young people little credit for the understanding they are capable of.

You can create ambition by empowering, intriguing, and inspiring the next generation.

Brie was a funny little kid, and her mother found it difficult to take her to work at their FOB. Unlike her accommodating big brother, Brie was always climbing, kicking, and tossing and rolling things around. Even the most understanding relatives would close their office doors when they saw Brie arriving with her backpack full of toys and Legos.

"Oh, Brie's been here," coworkers would note when they walked in and saw her stuff strewn about the conference room.

At four years old, Brie hauled worms around in a little red wagon, offering them for a penny each to passersby.

At five, she tried to sell friends her personally baked
clumps of dough, which she called "Sandcastles after the
Waves." By age nine, she was offering her services as an
in-home "distractor" for toddlers whose moms were pre-
paring dinner.

Brie's parents were aware that her conative strengths were probably
a mix of the Implementor/Quick Start initiatives. When Brie was
about 12, she completed the Kolbe Y(outh) Index and proved them
right. It explained her Implementor drive to create tangible products
and her Quick Start need to innovate rather than replicate.

Brie

Kolbe Y™ (Youth) Result

Fact Finder   Follow Thru   Quick Start   Implementor

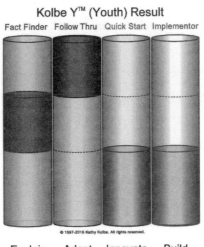

Explain   Adapt   Innovate   Build

It was clear Brie needed to figure out how to do her own thing, not
how to succeed within the existing FOB. As she grew into her teens,
the stuff in her backpack was sports equipment, along with the tools
conative adventurers need to carry with them.

Brie has learned to negotiate to gain the greatest possible freedom to do things her own way. Her parents have learned to shut her

bedroom door when she bangs on things dangling from the ceiling while she's listening to hard rock music.

Knowing what they knew about Brie's conative strengths, her parents encouraged her to learn about the pitfalls her Quick Start grandparent faced when founding the FOB, and to respect the needs of company employees who contribute other conative strengths. This awareness will help Brie if she opens her own FOB in the future.

The *Do*s and *Don't*s that make the biggest difference

As authors of this book, our mission is to help those who influence the next generation to instill in them a belief in themselves: in the difference they can make in the world, in the conative strengths they can always count on, in their ability to overcome obstacles that come from ignorance and prejudice, and in their right to fight for the freedom to be who they are.

What follows are guidelines we hope will help you share this mission.

DO DEVELOP CONFIDENCE, NOT ARROGANCE

Everyone has equal conative strengths, which come in a wide variety of MOs. No one has more of this instinct-based energy than anyone else does. But we all are more energized when we can do our own thing. And none of us is able to thrive when we have to work against our conative grain.

As terrific as it is for people to spend their life doing only what they're great at doing, it can give them the false sense that they possess more natural ability than other people. That, unfortunately, can result in arrogance, which also means a loss of humility.

Child prodigies can think "I'm the smartest person in the whole wide world," but if you ask them, "Can you play this sport well or can you write this story well?" they may not know the answer. It's not just in school: It's in hobbies, it's in giving different jobs at home so kids learn what they do and don't do well. (It is their conative instincts that drive the processes that either fit or don't fit their MOs.)

Learning humility is valuable for all employees, but young FMs who lack this trait when they enter the workplace can alienate their colleagues. Not only do they carry with them the burden of "royalty"; they act as though they're "to the manor born." The combination of being an FM and arrogant can make them impossible to work for . . . or with.

Humility comes from knowing yourself and understanding that since you can't do everything, you have to surround yourself with people who have a variety of differing conative strengths. It's tough to be humble, though, if you're afflicted by what we've identified as Arrogant Attitude Disorder (AAD). After kids are 12 or 13 years old, and they have AAD, they are much less likely to embrace humility than they would be if this problem had been identified and dealt with when they were younger. How do you knock down people at 18 or 28 or 38 who have been told they're the best and they're great, and they have won recognition for successes or been popular because they're handsome or star athletes?

When they fail in an FOB—and they will fail—they respond by saying or thinking "not fair" or "not my fault." Going through a failure from which others may bounce back can be devastating to a person suffering from AAD. Kathy relates this to something she observed on a soccer field.

> One of my grandsons played on a soccer team that became so good over years of playing together that they did not lose a single game for a couple of seasons. Much as I cheered for their victories, I became concerned that the expectation of them being winners could make the boys arrogant. It turned out to be good for them when

they finally lost a game, just before the playoffs. They needed that loss far more than a win. Did it help them win the championship? Well, at least it made them humbler winners when they did.

DON'T ACCEPT THE "I DUNNO" RESPONSE

One of the worst qualities in any employee is indecisiveness. It's ugly.

If you haven't taught your kids how to rate almost anything on a scale of 1 to 5, you better do it before you put them in a business environment—especially your own business. You may cope with their indecisiveness at home, where you might get exasperated, but you can shrug it off and move forward. But that doesn't work in the shop, at the trade show, or during a presentation.

Not making a decision is a decision. You're losing time, you're losing money, and you're losing credibility when an employee doesn't respond to a question with a sensible answer.

Recall from Kathy's conversation with six-year-old Sam (chapter 3) that one of the Kolbe "5 Rules for Trusting Your Instincts" is *Do Nothing—when Nothing Works*. That means you are deciding the time is not right to make a decision. Which is decidedly different from being indecisive.

How many decisions do you have to make in a day? On some days as FOB leaders we've counted over 50 decisions that we've had to make. It's clear, therefore, that family members who are indecisive are not ready to come into the business *at any level.*

If your child can't decide which Popsicle he wants, it's time you helped him learn to make choices. Start by offering choices among things you know he wants to do or things he wants to have. If he doesn't make immediate choices, give him what's left after you or others have eliminated options. Children who are used to having to decide what to order, what to wear, who to ask, when to change activities, and whether something is a good idea become decisive adults.

DO HELP KIDS PLAY TO THEIR STRENGTHS

One of the greatest gifts you can give children is confidence in using their instinctive strengths. Sometimes that requires that a parent encourage a child to do things in ways that wouldn't work as well for the parent. You met imaginative Brie earlier in the chapter.

> Brie's mother is the CFO of an FOB. The way she works best is through Initiating in the Follow Thru Action Mode. Her instinct is to plan ahead, using timelines, checklists, and regularized systems to achieve her goals.
>
> Dealing with a daughter who is all over the place was a challenge for Brie's mother. Child-rearing books tended to negatively label all the types of behaviors that she saw as her child's normal way of being. She knew she couldn't show her daughter how to succeed. She had no idea how to mentor Brie to follow her own instincts.
>
> No one in Brie's extended family had a kid like Brie. It helped that a coworker in the FOB did have experience raising a child whom she also had to prevent from being falsely labeled as ADD/ADHD. "I relate to what you're up against," the FOB's meeting planner told her. "Let me know if I can be of help."
>
> Brie's parents learned many tricks from the experience of the coworker.

Directing kids toward career options that will give them the freedom to use their conative strengths is the ultimate goal. That's why

Kathy spent years developing the Apt Careers program. It guides youngsters and adults toward careers that go beyond their interests. The career suggestions it gives are based on the conative strengths identified by the assessment within. These strengths are the essential ingredients to career success. Equally important, it tells you which careers among over 1,200 to stay far, far away from.

Just because there are jobs in an FOB that would give kids a chance to get work experience, don't put young relatives into them if those jobs don't fit their MOs. We've seen far too many kids not do well in such situations and develop fears about whether they could succeed in other jobs.

An FOB allows you to influence the levels of perseverance and persistence in the next generation. Rather than create special situations for kids with special needs, you can create options from which they can select what works best for them. This gives them the opportunity to rise to a challenge and experience the joy of figuring out how to accomplish the goals that have been set for them. And don't set those goals any lower for them than you do for others, or you will send the message that you don't think they can measure up to the others.

You may be surprised at how often special needs kids become the leaders who end up challenging others. They turn out to be among the most resilient kids because they have had to learn how to overcome so-called handicaps. That situation is quite different from making any child work against his or her conative grain.

DO LISTEN TO FUTURE FMS

Creative problem solving is not an age-related ability. Next-gen FMs may be able to solve problems as well or better than highly educated people who tell you that what the book says is the right answer. Because they haven't faced the same old problems, they don't have the same old answers.

Next gens know a lot more than you may think they do. They know a lot more about social media than most adults do, more about causes that may not interest you, more about contemporary shopping habits of youth, and more about how to dodge doing what you want them to do *just cuz you said so.*

Give them a chance. Seek their opinions. Have them rate products and services. Let them make some of your decisions.

> One of Ruth's grandsons, Michael, is especially adept with mechanical equipment and most technology. At 11, he was also a keen observer of all things on wheels, including cars. So, when Ruth wanted advice on purchasing a car, she asked him to help her choose the right vehicle.
>
> Even at his tender age, Michael had astute observations about the technical pros and cons. He noticed features that Ruth hadn't even considered. She was so impressed that at each car dealership they visited she told the salesman that Michael was the person he needed to convince. Two out of three car salesmen they spoke with at the different dealerships took her seriously and addressed him directly. Ruth and Michael walked away from the place where the salesman ignored her request. To this day, Michael ties that experience to a realization that his opinions mattered, and it gave him confidence to negotiate.

DO INCLUDE THE NEXT GEN IN PROFESSIONAL GROWTH OPPORTUNITIES THAT ARE UNIQUE TO FOBS

Take the members of the next gen to events at which they can see and hear relationship building, deal making, and commercial espionage in practice. Start when they're at an early age.

Shadowing FOB leaders at conferences, trade shows, sales calls, and vendor negotiations offers priceless educational value. If you keep it real, this will be far better than "take your child to work" activities that are often hokey.

What we've seen working best for introducing the next gen to their parents' work in an FOB is shadowing the parents (or grandparents) during important professional opportunities. The key to making it worthwhile is the prepping before the event and the debriefing afterward.

Incorporate all the questions shown below at some stage of your next-gen FMs' learning. The best way to use these as discussion starters is to know the conative strengths of the youngsters and to select the options that best suit their MOs. Here are some alternatives.

Fact Finder Initiators

- Observe the one-on-one discussions that take place on the sidelines. Who is doing it and why do they do it?

- Keep track of the people who you think are the most important decision makers in the room. Do they reach out to others, or do others come to them? Why?

- Is the time and money we spent at this meeting or event a good business investment?

Follow Thru Initiators

- Note whether we stay on the formal agenda, and whether some people take us off the agenda. If so, look for the pattern of who does it, and how they do it.

- Watch who listens and who does most of the talking. Does that factor predict who has the greatest impact on decisions?

- Does the design of the space assist the purpose of the

gathering? Will too many people sit at a side table and never mingle? Will too many cluster in front of the prototype, blocking the view of others?

Quick Start Initiators

- Pay attention to the words or expressions that trigger the most reactions.

- See if you can tell when someone is about to lose interest and either walk away or tune out of conversations.

- Do people who tell stories make them useful for their business purposes, or are they just entertaining others?

Implementor Initiators

- Pay attention to the ambiance. Is the music too loud for business conversations to take place without shouting? Is the lighting too low to see facial expressions from a distance?

- Consider all the physical space and quality issues, from air quality to seating layout. What impact could those issues have on our future decisions about attendance?

- Watch for the body language of individual attendees. Does it match what the person is saying? Does it give you any clues about their level of engagement?

Postevent discussions should involve answering these questions, then touching on the following topics. The type of answers given will depend a great deal on the MO of the next generation.

DON'T LIMIT FM INTERNS TO A
SELECT/NARROW GROUP OF JOBS

Good management of any business involves cross-training so employees can step into various jobs if others are absent. Methods developed for training new employees usually work well for training teenage interns. Those FM interns who are trained may well end up helping the company out during urgent situations. It also exposes them to career possibilities rather than just special project situations that are often given to interns.

By training teenage FMs for a variety of roles, it also helps remove the feeling of a "family cluster" in some parts of the business. FM employees and their offspring ought to avoid working in the same physical area, just as adult FMs should not work in close proximity, if avoidable.

FOBs may also "swap kids" in internship roles. "Your kid can work for me this summer if you can find a role for mine" is a nice offer—but only if you know that the other FOB shares your work ethic and other values. You may love your accountant, but his kid may lack ambition.

When you bring in FMs as interns, give them *real* work, not *busy* work. They are there to learn how to work, not how to regurgitate information.

DON'T HIDE THE REALITIES OF WORK FROM FUTURE FMS

Bringing future FMs in as interns with peers their age is an excellent way to engage your kids, grandkids, nieces, and nephews in efforts that can make a difference in your business environment. Be sure they understand the ground rules.

The FM internships at your FOB will be successful no matter what the age of the next generation if you follow these best practices:

- **Do** have them work toward a goal, not just observe.

- **Do** keep discussions professional, and avoid personal references.

- **Do** have them work with NFM interns when possible.

- **Do** give them age-appropriate assignments.

- **Don't** assume they know company jargon or culture.

While interns need to discover the joy of accomplishment, they also need to experience the reality that some parts of the work aren't as fun as others. At the end of the day, they benefit from a review of what they accomplished. Tracking their weekly goals is good for employees of all ages, but it's especially helpful with many of the younger kids (up through 18).

Don't hide economic realities from the next generation. Showing trust in a youngster's ability to handle exceptional situations in your FOB is a great confidence builder for both parties. As long as you have an optimistic outlook, especially during hard economic times, your younger family members will benefit from the experience of going through it with you. To build their resilience, expose them to financial situations that require a significant amount of creative problem solving. For example, help them learn to negotiate, to reschedule, to juggle priorities, and to do without.

Reality Checks: Questions to ask yourself

- ✓ Are you aware of the cognitive, affective, and conative strengths of next gens in your life?

- ✓ When the youth in your life encounter obstacles, are you encouraging them to deal with it rather than trying to handle it for them?

✓ When is the last time you asked for input from a next gen when making a decision?

✓ What opportunities have you given to the younger generation to observe a meeting, conference, or presentation?

✓ Have you recently openly shared concerns over a major FOB issue with next gens? If not, why not?

CHAPTER 9

Knowing When
Teams Won't Work

"My goal is to get everyone in our business working together in teams," a sports enthusiast said about his management style. "I know if I can do that, we'll beat out the competition—especially since we are a family of competitors."

Good luck with that!

We have never seen evidence of accounting departments improving profit and loss reporting methods by team brainstorming sessions; or programmers working more effectively by finishing each other's lines of code; or telemarketers getting more orders by having team members join in the conversation.

Some types of work (such as number crunching, car detailing, oil painting, book editing) are best done by individual contributors working independently—at least most of the time.

It's natural for FOBs to try to function as a team more than you would find in other enterprises. Often, FMs come into the business with experience interacting with one another, and they usually have a high level of trust and shared values. They assume a collaborative way of functioning.

> "We're great working as a team," Joyce says about herself
> and two siblings who all work in an FOB. "That's for sure,"
> her brother Duke says. "We grew up with a family room full
> of games and stuff we played with together. We're espe-
> cially into playing video games together."

Aside from the fact that Duke's examples pitted them against one
another, neither was building a good case for their having experience
working together to create sustainable solutions.

You don't have as much at stake playing Monopoly (even if you
play it for an entire weekend) as you do if you're acquiring a real piece
of property. When debt is real, many players end up working single-
mindedly on their own computations of the risks. Their individual
conclusions are essential to good problem solving. It's not a competition among them, nor is there time for collaborative discussion. They
need to run the data then compare their results to be sure they make
a wise decision.

We consider independent effort for the benefit of the company as
being different from collaborative effort.

Our work with Joyce, Duke, and their brother Wes led to the following conversation.

> "Why do you think it matters how we describe our team?"
> Joyce asked.
>
> Amy replied, "If you know you're a collaborative, inter-
> dependent team, you know the expectation is that you will
> wait for others to catch up if they get behind in some aspect
> of what you do. In your job, do you think it's important to
> wait for your brother to catch up?"
>
> "He's my brother, so I wouldn't leave him behind; but
> I get your point. At work it's different; if I finish what I'm
> doing, I'm free to move on to the next task. I never slow any

one down or let them slow me down. So I guess I actually am lucky not to work on a collaborative team."

"I love the team I'm on," Duke said. "We work coopera- tively, so if I get stuck, I can get my teammate to do the part of the project that is a problem for me, and I can help him out with something else. We're always going back and forth to each other's desks, or sometimes we all work around one of the big tables. It's so much more productive for us." (Interdependent team structures are most effective when collaboration is critical to a project.)

Wes worked on a team and with some of both charac- teristics. Sometimes he was out in the field working with clients, sometimes he was reporting back to his team about what he had found, and sometimes he was in the lab exam- ining specimens very closely with a partner who wrote down the findings.

"So where do I fit in?" Wes asked.

Wes is the epitome of a Hybrid Team member, which means he works both independently and interdependently. This is the most fre- quent form of functioning, especially in an FOB where FMs are a part of a family team but also could be working independently.

It is rare for employees in any kind of business to actually spend most of their time working collaboratively. Kolbe Leadership Analytics iden- tifies the three basic configurations in which people naturally work:

Collaborative Team efforts are seen when people

- Work interdependently
- Rely on one another's contributions
- Succeed through supportive, mutual efforts

Examples: software development team, basketball team

Independent Team efforts are seen when people

- Work separately as individual contributors
- Succeed by contributing individual excellence
- Come together mostly for reporting purposes
- Do not share space or work at the same pace

Examples: sales group, swimming team

Hybrid Teams are a combination of these and are formed when people need to switch back and forth between working interactively and independently in order to reach their shared goals.

FOBs are prone to place people on collaborative teams but also use them as individual contributors. You know your uncle is a great data analyst, but you also want him on the team that makes hiring decisions.

Examples: senior leadership group, baseball team

Why does it matter what type of team you're on?

If more business owners realized the differences in how Collaborative, Independent, and Hybrid Teams functioned, they would put better compensation systems in place.

> "You mean I would actually be paid based on my personal productivity—*not* based on the productivity of the combined efforts of a so-called team?"

That is exactly the point.

Because they work interactively, team members who are paid based on collective efforts can be helpful in generating more productive efforts from one another.

When a part or the whole of an organization forms a Hybrid Team, compensation and contributions vary over time. Recognizing this is the case, leaders schedule work, assign jobs, and give rewards with greater flexibility.

All of this matters in an FOB because of the stereotype of the family forming a team that excludes others. It ought never to happen.

These are essential guidelines that will help you create high-performance teams and avoid family cliques:

- **Do** assign teams that take advantage of the strengths of both FMs and NFMs.

- **Don't** let FMs form an exclusive team at work.

- **Do** provide reasonable options for people with special skills to work as individual contributors.

- **Don't** let yourself or others get stuck in isolated roles without options to participate on teams.

- **Do** be aware of the functional processes that drive your FOB, and advocate for fair compensation based on them.

- **Don't** confuse family familiarity with family working as a collaborative, interactive team.

Lead according to structure

If you are a leader, you need to give everyone you supervise some clarity on how you expect them to function. Then you need to manage them accordingly. Here are tips for leaders and others that will help each type function more smoothly:

> **Collaborative Teams** require assigning priorities and deadlines, which several people will work on together to achieve.

Members should be provided with resources they will share and be given time to sort out their roles. Members should be evaluated and rewarded for their combined results.

This is often easier to do with both FMs and NFMs on the team.

Independent Teams require defining individual responsibilities and required results. Members should each be given specific goals and be evaluated on their individual accomplishments.

This is far more difficult to do in an FOB because there are often assumptions of a greater need to work collaboratively no matter what the goal.

Hybrid Teams require flexible assignments and the ability to trade tasks as needed. Members often have to deal with working in a matrix, with a boss on two sides of the job assignments and evaluations. Compensation often works best as a salary for the team effort and bonuses for the individual work.

Managing and working in this environment can be highly rewarding, but the process is complex in an FOB. Both real and false assumptions concerning the reasons for FMs and NFMs having differentiated opportunities are bound to arise.

Team Synergy

A Collaborative Team composed of MOs that bring it the Synergy of differing instincts is likely to produce at least twice the levels of productivity as a non-Synergistic team. It gets more done. Members can trade off a task that might cause them to work against their own conative grain to someone who actually appreciates getting to do it. Even when they don't understand all the reasons why they work so well together, the balance in their approaches causes an energy flow that is self-sustaining. The following figure illustrates the team Synergy for a sample FOB. The MOs of each team member (FMs and NFMs) are used to measure the percentages for each of the 12 Action Modes.

Teams with Ideal Synergy get more done in less time, achieve more with fewer people, and need fewer financial and other resources to reach their goals. The ideal distribution of talents in such a team has variations in the percent of conative energy in each zone for each mode. However, our data shows that when the Action Modes are combined, the distribution of conative energy on a Synergistic team is distributed in a normal bell curve:

- 25 percent of the conative energy on the team Initiates action.

- 50 percent of the conative energy on the team ReActs.

- 25 percent of the conative energy on the team CounterActs.

Synergy Analysis

Kolbe A™ Distribution

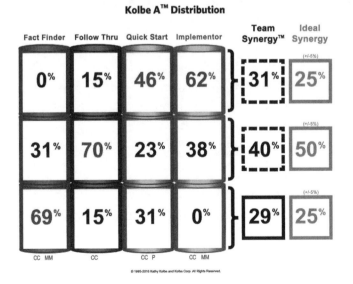

© 1995-2016 Kathy Kolbe and Kolbe Corp. All Rights Reserved.

But what's a leader to do if an FM believes that their family relationship earns them a position on the team, but their MO would mess up its Synergy?

Try telling your father-in-law that you'd really like him to join your project team, but he doesn't have the right stuff. You've got a problem—just like one of our recent clients had to face.

> Several high-powered executives in an FOB came back from an off-site retreat with very little to show for the time and money they spent.
>
> "What's the deal?" the CEO asked us. "You know these people are totally committed to this business and have the expertise to do what we needed to get done. But it didn't happen. I felt like I was dragging a moose through a swamp trying to get them to do any creative problem solving."
>
> When we looked over the data we had on the people they had invited to the retreat, the cause of the problem was immediately apparent.
>
> "You had the wrong mix of brilliant, experienced, highly committed people in the room," we explained. "Too many of them approach problems through the same Fact Finder method."

A Synergistic team has a balance of differing conative strengths among its members. When these abilities are used interactively, they provide an excellent mix of creative problem-solving methods. FOBs make a mistake when they give up Synergy for the sake of family peace.

They suffer additional losses of productivity if they fall into the trap of letting FMs pick other employees to work with on teams. It is yet another inappropriate way of putting family desires before business needs.

"Why can't Donny work with me?" his sister asked. "We love doing things together. We challenge each other to come up with better facts all the time. We'd get lots of information to help the company."

Of course they would, but Donny would be the fourth person on the team who is great at gathering data. That would cause inertia, which is a lack of forward momentum due to redundant ways of taking action.

It's easiest to work with people who do things the way you do them. It feels better when people agree with your methods. When your family owns the business, you may not have to justify your hiring and firing decisions as much as other businesses. You get more freedom to bring in people you want in it. So, you end up with groups of people who cause inertia in decision making.

Too many Initiating Fact Finders cause analysis paralysis on a team.

That's exactly what happened with the group that went to the retreat. They were people who found it easy to work together. If there is a lack of momentum, and your company seems stuck in a rut, inertia may well have snuck in. It naturally inhibits creativity no matter which Kolbe Action Mode is over-involved.

All too often, people want to go on adventures with those who share their MO, or ways of taking action. We urge you not to fall into that trap.

Too much Initiation in Follow Thru results in bureaucratic processes that bog down decision making. Imagine a government program run by a Collaborative Team composed mostly of Initiating Follow Thrus who create duplicate forms and copious procedures. (See chapter 1 to refresh your mind about the way all the Action Modes drive behaviors.)

Too many Quick Start Initiators cause chaos—kind of like a poorly moderated panel of political PR people on a cable TV show.

An abundance of handy Implementor Initiators slow down any project with a need to increase quality at any cost. It's great if you are going down white water in a raft—until it tips over. Then you better hope Initiating Follow Thrus packed the supplies and Initiating Quick Starts dive in and improvise solutions—which Fact Finders can assess as to the probability of success!

Because conative MOs are not genetic, second-generation FMs are rarely clones of their elders, but groups of friends do suffer from the cloning effect. If FMs hire too many friends, or hire people based on a desire to work with people who do things their way, they will create inertia. It is the single biggest reason for lost productivity in FOBs. Don't do it!

FOBs that survive to the third generation have gone through many situations that seemed like tumbling into raging rivers. Those that make it through the trip end up realizing the strength in conative differences.

Synergy isn't always comfortable, though.

The tug of war that happens between people who Initiate or CounterAct in a mode is a highly productive energy for problem solving. But, especially among FMs, it can feel like you're not playing "nice."

> "Why do you always have to put me down?" an Initiating Fact Finder says about the rolling of the eyes when she brings up the need for more data.
>
> "Well it's the same when you tell me that I don't know what I'm talking about just because I'm not a factoid."

Much as they love each other, they are at opposite ends of the continuum when it comes to the process of decision making. The company may benefit from their unique talents, but sometimes it feels as if their relationship is in danger. It takes understanding the three mental factors—thinking, feeling, doing (or cognitive, affective, conative)—to sort all of this out and leverage each other's differences.

Use open or closed spaces to fit the way people actually work

Interactive Team space, ideally, is open, with few walls. The team works in collaborative spaces designed to support its needs. Supplies are used exclusively by team members, and what's put on the whiteboards and flip charts stays there until team members alter it.

Independent Team space is easily recognizable by the rows of individual cubicles, and some large organizations have entire floors of them. Inside each is an independent contributor doing work that is often replicated by everyone in the area.

Hybrid Team space, at its best, is wide open, with portable furniture and movable walls. It includes shared meeting rooms and private work areas with flexible components, and it has clusters of workstations plus collaborative spaces. Workers have assigned spaces for their personal equipment, but they are pulled into the cluster areas as needed. Whiteboards are movable, and technology is sharable. Transportable equipment is signed out. No one assumes "ownership" of any of the space.

In any given area of an FOB, FMs should not work next to each other if possible. Few things anger NFMs more than an "undeserving" FM getting a plum space near another FM for no apparent business purpose.

Placing FMs throughout various office spaces also helps them keep an eye on things. They can make sure that no one is mishandling or stealing property, and they can also monitor the movement of employees: Is John spending too much time hanging out with Mary? Is Joan being a wallflower and failing to interact with people around her? Take egos out of it and give company needs the priority in assigning FM spaces.

Independent work can help team results

FOBs are often less formal in assigning roles than corporations are, especially for FMs. Regardless of the size of the company, the CEO may be conducting a senior staff meeting one minute and helping ready packages to be shipped the next. An FOB is structured according to a very basic rule: Do whatever it takes to get the job done.

> None of the FMs at the work site had seen Gloria for weeks. At first they thought she must be sick, but her brother said she was fine. "When she didn't show up during a very difficult phase of the project," her uncle said, "they were angry."
>
> Gloria had always been an important part of their team, so they had reason to feel abandoned. In fact, Gloria had been working independently on an innovative method for getting their work done more efficiently, with less danger. She got permission to work off-site on it, in secrecy, because the company wanted to protect the potentially marketable new system.
>
> "I feel like a jerk for not trusting Gloria," her uncle said. "I never thought of her as working just on her own. I thought she was too good for that. Ha! She worked on her own because she was good enough to figure out stuff when she wasn't working at the site."

Gloria needed to leave her usual team in order to do extremely important work. This doesn't mean that working independently makes a job more important. Her independent efforts did, in fact, make a significant difference for the entire organization. Gloria proved that as well, when she was able to help her team implement the new methods she had designed.

Recognize both individual and interactive contributions

Performance evaluations and compensation need to recognize the contributions of collaborative teams and individual efforts.

One of the most confounding problems among many FMs is the ever-present issue of which comes first, form or function. This affects lots of decisions, including titles, physical spaces, compensation, workload, and type of assignments.

What happens if you are lower on the family totem pole but have a function in the company that requires both working independently and showing high status to outsiders? Do you get a private office?

What happens when you have high status in the family but are not willing to work full-time in the business? Do you get a high-status role on a critical team yet not show up for most of the meetings?

Not unlike professors who claim authorship on research done by their students, business leaders do not always give credit according to where it is due. We find this is less likely to happen among FMs. Parents and grandparents who may have made the introduction are more likely to give credit to the next generation for closing the deal with a new client—even if that only involved doing the paperwork.

If you are an excellent individual contributor, but you work only occasionally on a highly collaborative team, should you get the bonus given to the team members? And a raise for your independent contributions, or just for your contributions on the team?

Answers to these questions often differ depending on the viewpoint of the contributor, team members, other FMs, and HR people.

The most unreliable answers in these circumstances are the actual "totem pole" ranking of fellow employees and 360-degree opinions of coworkers. Team members are not always fully aware of others' contributions. Even if they know the company asked several team members to have independent responsibilities, they would not be in a position to evaluate the actual impact of the work that was done.

HR professionals have generally not been savvy about the need to balance contributions from people who perform in hybrid environments. It is difficult enough to do performance evaluations in a matrix organization where an employee has two bosses: a line manager and a department manager, such as a tech support person assigned to the finance department but also rated by the tech manager.

In any business, being rated by peers is highly subjective. Some employees try to self-advocate. That puts everyone in uncomfortable situations in an FOB.

> Audrey's family knows the personal hardships she goes through because of her business travels. They are a part of the team that decides on bonuses and raises. That gives her an advantage over an NFM carrying the same load who may not have the same level of advocacy from others.

In a well-run FOB, decision makers are well aware of all these issues. They know that even the perception of a family bias could harm their employee relationships.

Despite gathering years of data relating to teams, we frequently come across FMs who believe their FOB experience is so different from all other FOB experiences that only they know what is right for it. Some of them make it work, at least for their generation. Some, like the CEO in this next story, find power is more important than people. That's far worse than inertia because he's the only person who can solve the problems he has created.

A multilevel marketing company started as a small FOB and has grown into a huge conglomeration of interrelated entities. FMs lead some of the companies and many of the divisions within them. At last count, there were more than 25 first- and second-generation FMs involved in it.

Hiro, the founder's son, is the CEO. He talks of the enterprise as being *one big team*. Of course, it isn't. It's impossible to have even the affective esprit de corps of an interactive team when differing subsidiaries are pitted against each other for both rewards and resources.

Everyone wants to be housed in the magnificent home office that includes child-care facilities, laundry services, ample parking, and a spectacular workout center. But half of the related enterprises are housed in relatively ordinary offices in other parts of the country.

Even the leadership team, which includes the presidents of all the entities, doesn't function collaboratively. They get together quarterly to discuss their operations, and have annual retreats with all their spouses. That hardly makes them an interactive team.

Hiro has what he calls his "family hotline," which is an as-needed teleconference with key FMs who work outside the home office. He told us this was a great way to make all of them feel a part of the family team. Again, any affective feelings of belonging that this may create do not translate into conative, action-oriented efforts that they take together.

So, are there problems here? The company is growing and employing lots of FMs and NFMs. What's to talk about?

Problems are lurking under the surface. Hiro's speeches about everyone working together as a big team ring false to many of the NFMs in the company, as well as to the FMs assigned to roles at a distance from the home office. To them, listening to Hiro's speeches and reading his directives doesn't really qualify as working interactively with HQ leaders.

The façade will crumble if Hiro doesn't give employees in the satellite offices benefits similar to those given to the employees at HQ. He also needs to realize that resentment is building on the part of NFM leaders who find out about changes in the businesses only after the FMs reporting to them hear about them on the family hotline.

As we write, Hiro is fighting off a "palace coup" of sorts. A brother has been chosen by dissidents within the FOB as the person they would support if he replaced his brother as CEO.

Hiro needs to remember that Business is Business. We have recommended that he discontinue his debriefs to all FMs (the Family Group). He started doing this in an effort to keep the family spirit alive inside a company that had long ago grown beyond what just FMs could manage. But, the conference calls inappropriately engage nonmanagement FMs in senior-management level business briefings. Instead, he could replace those calls with a purely social event such as a picnic or volunteer service activity with the FM families.

Of course, relatives, regardless of their percentage of ownership in the FOB, are entitled to written annual reports as well as all other information any owners are entitled to receive.

Hiro is learning the nature of true collaboration, but he has a long way to go to earn back the trust he needs in order to continue as CEO.

Reality Checks: Questions to ask yourself

- ✓ Are you trying to force FMs to work as a team when they would be more effective working independently?

- ✓ Are independent and interactive contributions recognized equally?

- ✓ Are you creating teams based only on FM relationships and not benefitting from the potential for instinctive team Synergy?

- ✓ Do NFMs have opportunities to be promoted over FMs in order to improve the overall functioning of a Hybrid Team?

- ✓ Are space and materials allocated to FMs based on their role in the organization and not their position in the family?

CHAPTER 10

Orchestrating Transitions

"Tell me you have a clever way of letting Uncle Cosmos know that he's being redeployed to Siberia," a client pleaded. We do. Simply put, he has to decide it's the best decision he ever talked you into making.

What makes transitions different in an FOB?

As much as you may try to follow the *Do*s and *Don't*s of separating business and family issues, every major transition in an FOB is likely to have an impact on some or all the FMs involved in it. There is a trickle-down effect that affects the spouses, children, and grandchildren of those directly involved in the business.

In an FOB there is usually one person or a small group of people who cause transitions that impact many other FMs. Transitions are, by nature, disruptive. If the people who will be most affected are involved in the decision-making process, you have won half the battle. If they are encouraged to focus on what will stay the same, you have won the other half.

Yet FMs who aren't in senior decision-making positions don't necessarily have the big picture, possess all the facts, or understand the impact a transitional decision may have. There is a lot of pressure on the FM who makes most of the decisions.

All FMs need to have some perspective about and appreciation for how hard it is for FOB leaders to understand that they cannot make decisions that make everyone happy. Some FMs feel blindsided when major decisions are announced that they hadn't known about. They mistakenly think they should have been given a say. Business is Business, however, and an FOB leaders' responsibility to the business is different from their responsibility within their families.

When Steve, the son who was running the family farm, announced to his parents that he wanted to turn it into a regional entertainment destination—with a restaurant, an outdoor arena for shows, a petting zoo, and other attractions—they were flabbergasted. They had never envisioned such a dramatic transition. Going from farming the land to becoming an entrepreneurial entertainment center? Was he risking their retirement money as well as doing something that would change their lifestyle?

Steve's wife knew he was troubled by the farm's declining revenue and increasing expenses. She was well aware that keeping the family farm going was getting more and more difficult. But his big plans seemed too risky—too huge a transition.

Steve's kids loved the idea, but they had no concept how much the transition would affect their daily work: from helping to feed the animals and collect the eggs, to taking tickets, to running around trying to wave people into open parking spaces.

Steve's siblings would also not be able to enjoy doing the work they had been raised to do well. Those who didn't work on the farm would miss coming around for quiet picnics.

Steve had acquired most of their shares in the property, yet he kept many of them employed, which had seemed a good idea. If it weren't for the history of it being an FOB, no one would have questioned his freedom to do with it as he wished now that he owned most of the land.

But question it they did. Most of his family did not think he should feel free to transform the farm into an entertainment center.

"He can't do that!" his sister exclaimed to their mother.

"Yes, he can dear," she said. "No one is sadder than I am that he thinks this is a necessary change. But, I respect him for being able to move forward and make the land useful. Don't judge him by how well he holds on to the past. Give him a chance to prove how he can make this work."

If there had been a family vote, Steve would have lost. Transitions in an FOB rarely come through consensus, or even a general understanding of all the issues that are involved in making significant transitions.

By following the guidelines you've read in the previous chapters, you will facilitate the transitions you need to make in your business. Whether these major changes involve promotions, reorganizations, or mergers and the like, the *Dos* and *Don'ts* we've discussed will help your transitions proceed more smoothly than they otherwise might. In fact, when we talk to clients who have observed these guidelines, they describe how potentially difficult shifts in their FOBs proceeded without as much pain and stress as they had initially feared.

When it comes to the transition of turning over a business to another FM, shared values are a prerequisite. Knowing that the next person in charge shares your values will help you become more comfortable when you hand over your cause, your business, "your baby." When we've asked people why it worked so well for them to merge with another company, or turn the business over to the next generation, their answers centered on values:

- "It was seamless because we all shared the same sense of purpose."

- "There was never any doubt that we were on the same page about the mission."

- "They did things differently, but they would stick to the same principles about why they were doing it."

In contrast, here's what we've heard when transitions don't go well:

- "The partners we brought in didn't share our belief in quality. They were all about profit. We couldn't let them erode customer confidence in our long-standing product promises."

- "He was smart and had everything going for him, except he didn't get how much we valued team efforts. He thought he could 'phone it in.' People didn't respond well to that. They worked collaboratively . . . to show him up. And he opted out."

- "I thought I had raised my daughter to value loyalty, but when I gave her the reins, one of the first things she did was eliminate the roles of people who had been with us for decades. It broke my heart."

An especially difficult situation involved a father and daughter who had both assumed that she would take over the business when her dad turned 65.

We watched Margot defy her father when it came to hiring guidelines. He believed in only hiring people who had the striving instincts needed for the job. Margot had hired friends without having them go through their standard process, so she didn't know if they had the conative MOs that fit the roles she put them in. Bypassing these procedures caused her to lose the respect of many employees. She put the company at risk in not abiding by their otherwise consistent hiring practices and by the problems caused by the misfit hires.

When her dad passed over Margot and brought in an outsider to replace himself as CEO, she told him, "I can't imagine that you think it is appropriate to give the CEO position to an outsider when you have an experienced daughter sitting right here."

"Margot," he said, "I can't imagine that you think it would be appropriate for me to pass the baton to someone who has ignored our core value regarding fair hiring practices. Business is Business. You made it clear that you put friendships first. I hope someday you prove that you share the company values and can be put in the top leadership role."

How conative strengths determine outlooks on transitions

You have a huge advantage when you navigate through major changes in an FOB if you understand the conative part of your mind as well as the MO of others. It helps you anticipate and address how a given FM is likely to respond to any type of transition. For instance, you can predict that Follow Thru Initiators and Quick Start CounterActors who were left out of the decision process will have natural highly negative reactions. These are the types of things we hear them say:

Follow Thru Initiator: "What? You are expecting me to stop the work I'm doing before it's finished? I deserve the right to clean it up and put it in a box with a bow on it. Without that kind of closure, everything I've been doing will have been a waste of time and effort. Just let me finish it, and then we can discuss the next thing you want me to do."

Quick Start CounterActor: "There is no way I'm going to jump into a new role before I have time to figure out how it impacts my future. There are too many uncertainties in the way you've described it. It's not going to work if I can't use the experience I've gained."

For Initiating Quick Starts, who usually force change, negative reactions coming from people they love can hurt deeply.

"What most of the family didn't realize," an FOB partner said after a business-altering merger, "was that we were enhancing their future opportunities, both for jobs and income. All we got from the other family members were ignorant rants."

The struggle between those who Initiate change and those who try to CounterAct or prevent change can get very emotional, but the energy behind the tug of war is conative. Those who react through mid-zone modes can get whiplash trying to go back and forth between people at odds over how to deal with change.

Initiating needs for each Action Mode

- Fact Finder—needs all the justifications for doing it

- Follow Thru—needs to create a plan for worst-case scenarios

- Quick Start—needs to incite change and be challenged by uncertainties

- Implementor—needs to walk through space and equipment

CounterActing needs for each Action Mode

- Fact Finder—needs to help simplify the advantages

- Follow Thru—needs to maintain flexibility and take advantage of random opportunities

- Quick Start—needs to be certain what aspects of the business will stay the same

- Implementor—needs to deal with the abstract, concentrating on envisioning what it's going to be like

Beyond these Action Modes, a number of other factors affect how well people handle transitions. Moving the location of an FOB home office is a much bigger deal for those in a family enterprise than for those in other businesses because FMs are more likely to have sentimental feelings about the years they worked there, especially if they founded it. Similarly, a move can create jealousy when the new location is nearer to one part of the clan than another, or if it results in a move to a suburb from the city (or vice versa) and some FMs feel the new location is a slap in the face of tradition/culture.

Transitions in policy can be disruptive if the value that drives them is not clear, if they are not implemented on an ethical basis, or if they are not communicated well to everybody involved. For instance, it's common to change or take away benefits as a company grows and matures in order to be fairer to all employees. FMs can be particularly resentful if these needs are ignored, and they may take the change in policy or benefits as personal insults.

Here are some examples of what we've seen over the years:

- Eliminating paid internships to FMs under the age of 18. "What! Why aren't the younger FMs getting the same benefits as their older siblings?"

- Taking away FMs' favored status for parking spaces in order to base parking on seniority within the business.

"Way to make the next generation in the family feel disrespected!"

- Making tickets for sporting and other events available only to full-time employees. "Great. I work for years to build the company for the next generation, and now that I have time to enjoy some of the day games, they aren't available to me."

- Determining the number of vacation days on years of full-time work, not years employed. "My work at the family business had to be part-time for a few years so I could get insurance benefits that we couldn't afford for our employees. Later, I took time off to get the advanced education that would help the company. Now I'm going to be penalized for those decisions."

These policy decisions were usually made by the new generation of leaders. In one of these cases, a third-generation CEO decided that no more than one person from any family could work in any department in the company, and the following argument ensued.

"Grandma and grandpa worked together to start this place," another FM said angrily, "but now some consultant has warned us that two family members can't work together productively? That's just wrong!"

Business is Business. But in a non-FOB, if a business decision harms you, you can complain to everyone you know (and expect sympathy)—or just quit.

When the business is an FOB, you have to be careful what you say, and to whom. As an FM, you are supposed to try to understand the decision makers' point of view. You can't just quit without being judged by other FMs. The bridges you burn are far more important than the loss of a job or a job reference. They are the bridges to your home and hearth.

Involve key influencers before announcing transitions

Key influencers for the FOB may not even be FMs. It is often helpful to have the perspectives of NFMs; their broader experiences and their awareness of family values are useful.

A key influencer could be the no-nonsense, military officer son-in-law who will tell others to "suck it up," helping others recognize that sometimes a leader has to send the troops into combat for the good of the whole. It could also be the retired schoolteacher aunt who says, "I never had a primo parking space in all the years I taught. Get over it!"

Or you might hear from the sibling who runs her own successful business.

> "You've gotta be kidding me. You can't just rule by edict in this business, even if you are the founder and majority owner. You got help from FMs when you needed them to drop everything and come to work for you. You made all of us your guinea pigs for your product development ideas. This isn't just about money. This is about family loyalty. Figure it out so you make everyone whole—or at least so they know you did everything you could to make that happen."

Of course, you can also get input from outside consultants who have experience working with FOBs. Recognize, though, that some of these consultants have never personally experienced deep involvement in the emotional aspects of FOBs. Hiring these types of consultants is similar to taking a course on entrepreneurial decision making from a university professor who has never taken the risk of running a business.

Don't confuse next-generation changes with changes in values

Don't let your confidence in the strength of the family keep you from seeing economic and other realities that could erode the company's viability.

All FMs need to continually review the progress and obstacles they see for the company and their responsibilities within it.

Conventional wisdom is that the older generation needs to pass things along to the next in good shape, but the responsibility is also on the next generation to be ready to take charge. That means understanding how the FOB works and learning management skills. It involves working well with all employees, including NFMs, with whom they need to collaborate at all times—especially during major transitions.

It's difficult for a new CEO to come into a large public corporation and affect the culture of the organization because CEOs often come and go quickly. CEOs of FOBs, on the other hand, tend to lead them for 10 or 20 years. A new FM leader can come in and dramatically change the entire culture. Recognize the next generation's need to put its own stamp on the company. Maybe this even includes redecorating or changing how meetings are run. Sometimes it may include rebranding or changing the company's logo. When going through these radical cultural changes, be careful to preserve continuity among your clients or employees; otherwise, you could lose their confidence.

Plan for worst-case scenarios

Transitions caused by natural disasters have wiped out a surprisingly large number of businesses. When they happen in the hometown where an extended family has an FOB, it can damage their business and homes in one blow. Contingency plans for keeping the business working and protecting records should be a constant consideration.

If a flood closes your retail store for an extended period, FMs on commission will suffer financially along with FM executives who are unlikely to get bonuses or raises. FMs and their families are likely to pitch in and spend most of their waking hours cleaning out the debris. It's another good news/bad news aspect of being an FM working in an FOB. How great to work as a team to save the business. How horrible to have so many of you hurting financially at the same time.

> When a tornado made a wicked path through a midwestern county, many members of an extended family were injured, their homes lost, and both of their large FOB auto dealerships were badly damaged. It took every resource they had to help all their employees during a time when there was no inventory to sell, no place from which to sell, and no staff, because most employees were engaged in caring for their family and homes. Was their transition going to be closing down the business, rebuilding it in one or both of the locations in the same county, or starting over in another business, perhaps in another place?
>
> Help was available for a few weeks, and then volunteers moved on. Insurance covered a fraction of the material losses—and, of course, none of the emotional ones.

In situations such as these, FMs have often realized how much a part of their family many NFM employees have become. They suffer, too, but they continue to try to help the business as best they can. There are no insiders and outsiders when the walls have been torn down, figuratively and literally, by nature.

The tragedy of the sudden loss of a founder or FM leader can cause a terrible disruption in an organization. Other types of tragedies can take key players away too. A dramatic example is the 9/11 attack, when several FMs, who were partners in financial services firms, died unexpectedly.

Having legal and financial advisors assist in transition strategies and succession plans is critical for an FOB. During a crisis, we suggest to FMs they Do Nothing—when Nothing Works. Take time to take care of each other. Accept what help others are able to provide. Don't even try to make any but the most basic business decisions until you have some separation from the crisis and can think clearly.

Fortunately, facing change caused by horrible disruptions causes many organizations—FOBs or not—to come together. Human beings have a wonderful way of nurturing each other through losses. For a while after tragic events, everyone is blessed to have caring people around them. In an FOB the nurturing lasts longer than in other organizations, and the FMs and NFMs pull together as a team.

A couple of years after she had turned the business over to the next generation, Kathy was staying in the mountains a couple of hours away from the home office. She was up late at night working on a new project when her son David, the company's CEO, called.

"Mom, are you sitting down?"

"Oh, nooooo!" Her mind raced through the locations where she believed family members might be at that hour.

"David, just tell me what's going on."

"The office is on fire."

"Oh, thank God!" she said. To her, Business is Business. When it comes to a crisis, better it be the business structure than a family member or the home of a family member that's in danger.

"I'm here talking with the fire department. It looks like a total loss," David said.

"Okay. I know you and Amy will do whatever needs to be done," she said, realizing that as chairman of the board, she needed to reconfirm that with him. "We're planning to be back in town in a couple of days. Send me photos if you get time."

Kathy felt no need to question the FOB's next-generation leaders about how they would handle the loss of the building that had housed the company for over 30 years.

As often happens in a crisis, it was an opportunity for FMs and NFMs to band together to do more than recover from the fire; they worked long hours in cramped quarters while moving the office and creating a wonderful new environment for fulfilling the mission of the company.

Power struggles lead to transitions

Weaknesses can appear as leaders of an FOB manage the aftermath of disasters or deal with poor business cycles. A downturn in the economy, a failed new product line, a union strike; anything that interrupts the flow of business causes people within it to question their own and others' decision-making abilities:

"Sorry, guys," said a longtime client of ours. "I know how much you value family sticking together. I just can't continue

to watch my Aunt Anita put cheesy products in our cata-
logs. For the good of the brand, I've decided to challenge her
dictatorial decisions."

"I thought Nick was just great as senior partner, until I saw
him totally mess up the negotiations. The strike was his
fault," said his brother, an FM who was also at the partner
level. "It made me realize it was time for us to remove him
from that key role."

"Watch out! I've had it!" said another client. "That's the
last board meeting I'm going to where all the FMs defer to
Mr. Big Shot. He may be the eldest of us, but he's also the
dumbest. I've gotta pay for my kids going to college, and at
the rate he's spending all our money, there won't be enough
to go around."

Often, the critics in the family have good reasons for their frustration, anger, and fear. In these transitional situations, access the levels
of shared values, the levels of trust, and the levels of effort that all the
FMs share—or not.

If there have always been problems relative to values, trust, or
effort, it is certainly time to make changes. Usually, someone has to
go. The power struggles come into effect if there needs to be a shift in
power but there is no agreement on what that shift looks like.

Job security in FOBs

It's no secret that FMs have more job security than other employees in
an FOB do. Yet, if they leave it, their one-company résumés and lack
of diversity in their experiences can make them less likely to thrive in

the job market. That's good news for the FOB that needs long-term stability, but it's a problem for both FMs and the business when it needs shaking up from the inside.

Low turnover is usually highly desirable in any business. But every business needs to turn over employees who are not cutting it. It is tough to fire an FM, and corporate HR people can find it difficult if they have to build a case against an FM.

> Over cocktails one evening, an FOB founder confided in a close friend, "The business would be better off if it were leaner and meaner, but I can't lay off FMs. I try hard to get them training and opportunities to develop skills so they could find good jobs in other places. A couple of the best of them have moved on to great careers outside the business, but I am saddled with a few other FMs who will end up retiring here."
>
> "Sorry, pal," the friend responded. "From the outside, it's been easy to see this coming. I guess you just never wanted to acknowledge it."

What keeps FMs awake at night?

Anyone consulting or coaching leaders of FOBs knows the answer to this question. These are the ways we've heard it said most often.

> "The one thing that makes me hate being in a family business is when the problems with a family member cause us to have to let him go."
>
> "Let him go" is a strange way to describe what is most commonly known as "firing" or "terminating" an employee.

There are no good words for this situation. It stinks to have to tell anyone they're no longer wanted or needed. It is particularly awful to have to do it to an FM.

> "I heard you had to lay your sister off. How did it go?"
> "How do you think it went?!"

There is no such thing as it going well.

If you are the person who has to remove an FM from the payroll, your goal always needs to be to get that person to decide to leave.

If you are the FM whose performance gets criticized a lot, your goal should be to find a way to do what needs to get done or find a healthy and professional way to leave. You may know that others think you are doing a poor job, but you may not know what to do about it.

> "It's not my fault. She's a terrible manager. There's no way to please her."

We've heard this from employees who think their boss is to blame for their poor levels of productivity. But the boss says that no matter how she tries to manage the complainer, he doesn't seem to be able to get the job done.

The business needs must be met. Both sides of the equation have to be analyzed. There has to be a resolution to the problem.

When looking at the situation objectively, patterns become apparent. If the manager is the problem, productivity problems will also exist with other people she manages. If the FM is the problem, a good manager will have records that provide objective evidence to prove it.

Many FOBs have a bad habit of not having appropriate measurements of productivity or a process to assure that the ones they do have are applied equally.

"We know when it's working and when it's not. We don't need all that HR, C.Y.A. stuff around here."

Yes, you do. The best way of "getting rid of the bad apples" in an FOB is to be as objective as possible. And as kind as you ought to be.

One way to effectively evaluate whether to invest time and effort into retaining the FM is to analyze the person's contributions from the perspective of all three mental factors. Deciding whether you can fix performance issues always comes back to considering the FM's fit for the business.

Ask yourself the following questions:

- **Cognitive**: Does the FM have the capabilities to do the job? If not, does he or she have the capacity to gather the skills or knowledge necessary?

- **Affective**: Does the FM share the company values? Are there personality or motivational differences that can't be changed?

- **Conative**: Does the FM have the conative strengths that match the needs of the position? If not, can we find a better fit for the FM elsewhere in the business? Is the FM giving an appropriate level of effort to his or her work?

As much as you want to make it work with a problem FM, if your instincts say it never will, trust your instincts:

- **Do** be specific about poor performance issues as they happen.

- **Don't** wait for problems to fester before figuring out how to help the low performer.

- **Do** analyze whether the problem is caused by cognitive, affective, or conative issues.

- **Do** provide a mentor/coach/trainer (often an NFM) or classes to help the FM beef up skills or knowledge.

- **Don't** put up with a bad attitude.

- **Do** try an "attitude adjustment" discussion if a bad attitude is the problem.

- **Do** confirm that the FM is being given an opportunity to fully contribute his or her conative strength. If not, change the role.

- **Don't** tolerate low levels of conative effort.

- **Do** provide professional help, if necessary.

If you are an FM feeling embattled in the process of trying to save your job,

- **Do** ask management to go through the *Do*s and *Don't*s listed in this chapter that apply in your situation.

Real solutions, as opposed to going through the motions, involve open dialogue and sincere high-level efforts by *all parties who are involved*:

- **Don't** turn to relatives who are outside the FOB for help. That clearly crosses the line. Business is Business. They are not a part of it, so keep them out of it.

Reality Checks: Questions to ask yourself

✓ Is respect shown for the different ways people instinctively deal with transitions?

✓ Do all FMs have an appropriate say in potential changes in the FOB?

✓ During major transitions, are the needs of NFMs considered equally to those of FMs?

✓ How difficult is it to separate family-related emotional issues when dealing with business changes?

✓ Do you turn unplanned transitions into positive opportunities?

CHAPTER 11

Graceful Exits

Finding a graceful exit from an FOB takes as high or higher a level of effort as the work you put into it.

It takes a longer view of the purposes of the business for founders to willingly step aside for the next generation. When founders think it through and decide to take charge of the destiny of the FOB, as well as their own destiny, it reduces the stress for everyone. They can begin the next exciting chapter rather than end the story.

"You've been such a major part of this company. You can't leave," is a compliment—and a challenge. Every FOB leader has to leave at some point. The more you care about the FOB's purpose and the people in it, the more thought you need to put into how to step out.

> "He was our best CEO in three decades, but we had to let him go at the height of his career because we have a drop-dead aging-out clause in his contract" is an actual quotation from the chairman of the board of a major company.

FOBs change rules rather than make that kind of stupid mistake. They make other mistakes, though. Mostly, they avoid bringing up the touchy subject of FMs needing to move on.

It's usually up to the person who should depart to figure out how to do it. Few FMs have experience doing that.

> Linda's husband kept changing their product offerings and buying new businesses instead of maximizing their current asset—the family manufacturing company. He became especially bored with day-to-day business during periods of slow growth. Tightening his belt, holding down expenses, and waiting it out were not this Quick Start Initiator's forte.
>
> Linda was the person within the company who gave it stability. When the company's financial situation was so dire, and her husband had almost completely lost interest in it, she stepped up and formally took over the leadership. The transition was hard on everyone, FMs and NFMs alike.
>
> While Linda kept the company solvent and even increased profits, the newfound way of success bred animosity with her husband and many other members of the family. They were comfortable with the old business structure, in part because Linda had smoothed things over when they really weren't working as well as it seemed.
>
> It nearly destroyed some relationships when it seemed to them that Linda had usurped power from her husband for reasons they imagined were far more devious than was true. Linda was the only person who recognized the problems and faced them head-on. She knew what had to be done and did it. Others were aghast by what seemed an unnecessary power grab.

You can prevent the trauma of essential transitions in an FOB by fostering an acceptance of the natural need for adjustments in the roles within it. Dads always stay dads, but they don't always stay the leader of the FOB.

It's comfortable to continue family traditions, but traditions can kill the FOB. The business always needs to be agile. Its leaders need to adjust to opportunities and changes in the marketplace, technology, and laws. When FMs become unable to perform well in the FOB, they have to switch roles or give up their role in the business. That should never change their role in the family.

Seeing humor in the process of "letting go"

Here's an example of how letting go wasn't always so easy for Kathy.

A few months after Kathy turned management of Kolbe Corp over to David Kolbe and Amy, she stopped by Amy's office one day. Amy was about to start a lunchtime staff meeting, so she asked Kathy if she would like to stay for pizza.

Having run similar meetings for years, Kathy began to question the variety and quantity of pizza Amy had chosen.

Amy admitted later she was ticked. How badly did Kathy think a next-generation successor could screw up the pizza order? Was she truly ready to let go if she couldn't even trust the president she chose to get the right amount of pizza without any meat?

This turned out to be a great way to distinguish between the type of decisions Kathy needed to trust her son and daughter with, and the type that she still needed to teach them about. Trusting their judgment about small decisions was clearly different from their need to continue to learn key historic information that would help them with more critical ones.

Amy: We knew she fully trusted us to run the business when we got to the point where we all thought it was funny to call Kathy out for giving "pizza-level" advice. So, we often joke about the level of decision by asking whether it is a pizza-level decision.

Kathy has shared that the toughest situations for her were when she believed that her experience could prevent harm to the company, but Amy and David didn't see her point. Those weren't just intellectual arguments from Kathy's point of view. She was aware of a reality that her successors had not yet faced, and this was a case when they weren't trusting the founder's advice. At Kolbe Corp it hasn't happened very often, but when it has, the stakes were very high.

In those situations, the founder has to choose between outcomes that could harm the business or a process that could harm the FM relationships.

Forget the pizza ordering.

How founders and FOB leaders can exit gracefully

Founders who leave leadership roles should leave the building. When FOB founders voluntarily step down, there are two things to prove: that they can stay away and that the next generation can take over.

Removing themselves from the day-to-day operations helps FOB leaders stay out of lower-level decision making. This can be the hardest part of the transition in the beginning.

Only people who have never done it think this happens overnight. The flow of information needs to continue. "Picking the brain" of the founder should be a welcome opportunity for all involved. Continuing to communicate is essential for maximizing the intellectual capital of the business.

Founders won't leave the next generation in the lurch if they have worked together to do the necessary knowledge transfer long in advance of the actual changing of the guard. All the *Dos* and *Don'ts* in the previous chapters of this book are stepping-stones leading to this period in the business.

What a founder did, no one else in the business can ever do. But then, these are things that no one else ever needs to do again.

A healthy transition does not just happen in one day, and the leaving of the building ought not to be a jarring event. Founders need transition periods during which they are away from the office. This can include personal or business travel, community projects, working from home. This assures space for the new leadership to be in charge.

Founders may continue to touch base with the FOB after they have officially left as long as it's for the sake of the new leaders and not their own personal needs. It is their responsibility to have found ways to use their conative abilities productively so that they don't use those visits for self-gratification. For example,

- If you're fully retired, then only go back for social functions, etc.

- If you're still an owner or board member, go back as needed by the FOB, not by your personal desire to be otherwise involved.

Prevent ugly exits

Some founders have a strong feeling of entitlement, and they fear the empty office as much as some fear the empty nest. Helping them transition out can be tremendously difficult.

Such transitions are easier if you've built a case for it over time, and you've openly discussed how it is a part of the life of the business. Every FM has to have some awareness of the probability of how things might look in the future.

Play out worst-case scenarios about how things may or may not work. Don't make long-term promises for FM employment. All your discussions about putting family relationships first will come back to bite you if there is not a reality-based understanding as well as documentation of the fact that no one has a lifetime guarantee of employment in your FOB.

*Do*s and *Don't*s for FOB leaders

- **Do** decide, while you're healthy and full of energy, at what stage will it be appropriate for you to hand over the reins.

- **Don't** wait for people or circumstances to force you out.

- **Do** give credit where credit is due to the next generation.

- **Don't** think you're the only person who can keep the place going.

- **Do** openly discuss your plans for the future.

- **Don't** leave the next generation wondering what in the world you're thinking.

- **Do** have friends outside the business with whom you enjoy spending time.

- **Don't** make the business your entire life.

- **Do** send occasional articles or reminders to the office.

- **Don't** stop by for unscheduled meetings.

- **Do** things that make you happy.

- **Don't** stop being productive.

Dos and *Don'ts* for the next generation

- **Do** empathize with the founder's fears of becoming irrelevant.

- **Don't** minimize the contribution they could still be making.

- **Do** encourage them to find their own outlets for their experience and energy.

- **Don't** suggest things you would do if you were in their place.

- **Do** everything you can to make sure you don't face too many financial unknowns.

- **Don't** make too many financial promises the business can't afford.

- **Do** welcome former FOB leaders when they show up in the office.

- **Don't** alter workflow while they are there.

- **Do** seek out the founder's advice when it could be helpful.

- **Don't** hesitate to seek advice because you think it might make you look weak.

- **Do** put your own stamp on the business.

- **Don't** change everything that made it successful.

Moving forward

People often ask how we, at Kolbe Corp, made such a smooth transition from Kathy running it to David and Amy being in charge. Here's Kathy's perspective as the founder of an FOB, a wife, and a mother.

It's important to emphasize that we spent years together learning to use most of the *Dos* and *Don'ts* in this book. As Quick Start Initiators, we used the trial-and-error method with many other *Dos*—some of which turned into *Don'ts*. We've trusted David's conative MO that combines Fact Finder initiatives and Quick Start ReActions to keep the strategic balance.

Hindsight allows us to include here what worked for us and for hundreds of other FOBs we've observed. While there were mistakes along the way, our sharing of values and our mutual trust has been the solid foundation for our productive collaboration.

On a day in 2001, when I was working in my home office, completely absorbed in writing material for Kolbe Corp, I got a call inviting me to lunch with David, Amy, and Will. Since we had a tradition of birthdays-only lunches with just family, I figured this would involve some kind of intervention or sharing of serious news.

David opened the discussion with their truly kind offer for me to take a sabbatical, "to do whatever you would like to do, for as long as you want to do it." They knew I was frustrated and thought one issue was my not having taken many vacations over the years. They wanted to give me the opportunity to make up for that. It could have been Will and me sailing around the world together or my taking courses at Harvard. The thought of doing either made me laugh.

I didn't want time off. I wanted time to do what matters most to me, and to do it in my way, which includes CounterActing Fact Finder—which is not usually welcome in the standard academic/corporate/political world.

I loved the idea of my being free do to anything I wanted to do. What I wanted to do was start a new business, an enterprise that would allow me to build a small team that could focus on my primary missions: using my theory of conation to improve patient care and career assessments and opening a brain research center dedicated to studying the interrelationships of all three domains of the brain.

It surprised me that they seemed so relieved. And, as Amy put it, it surprised them that I said yes immediately. They assumed that I would feel too responsible for oversight of the company to spend much time away from it.

I told them I would appreciate a break from Fact Finder writing, especially on topics I had been explaining and re-explaining for years. What I didn't know yet was what I would miss.

David, Amy, and Will thought it would take me a couple of weeks to tie up loose ends. I wanted it to start immediately. And so it did, two days later. We kinda sorta agreed on a three- to six-month hiatus.

Within a few days of my having the total freedom to do whatever I decided was most important for me to do, I called up David and Amy and told them, "I'm not coming back. There's no need for me to do that. I totally trust the two of you to run Kolbe Corp, and my Quick Start/Follow Thru needs to plan projects for the future."

We quickly agreed that I would continue to be chairman of the board and part of the team that coteaches our Kolbe Certification classes and annual continuous learning programs. I also wanted to coauthor books and products with them. As the author of most of the intellectual property Kolbe Corp publishes, I would retain the right to continuously improve those products and programs and approve their efforts to do the same. It was comforting that Will was there as the keeper of the history, and fact-checker for proper use of the language of the theory, along with his client work.

During this transition I didn't have an office at Kolbe Corp HQ. Trying to stay out of the way, yet instigate Quick Start projects, put me in conative stress. It wasn't productive for me to ask Amy if she had put in the appropriate pizza order, and there were lots of other ways that it didn't work for me when I had one foot in the business and one foot out the door.

It was not easy to stop jumping in with ideas for Kolbe Corp marketing or suggestions for handling PR opportunities. We agreed that I would go through Amy to do that. In that, I was a slow learner. Correction: I'm not there yet.

David is both an attorney and Wharton Business School alum. We both know there is a natural conative conflict between us. Knowing it doesn't make it go away, however. It was clear that the more I stayed away, the less the conflict would get in the way.

I was blessed that both Amy and David were doing a great job in roles that fit their cognitive, affective, and conative attributes and that they have an amazingly wonderful team. It has been a joy to watch them grow into very fine leaders.

For all founders, the trick is to have someplace to go. I've moved on to develop a terrific new team and to help develop new projects, in a different FOB.

Done and done. And we've never had to change the deal that has worked well ever since.

Reality Checks: Questions to ask yourself

If you are a founder of an FOB,

- ✓ Have you thought about what you will do to make good use of your mental skills, affective interests, and conative strengths when it is time to turn the business over to others?
- ✓ Do you check in with outside advisors to be clear about your capabilities and the realities of your thinking about when and how to exit the FOB?
- ✓ Have you identified the people you can trust to take over the leadership, and are you giving them the opportunity to prove their capabilities?
- ✓ Are all potential successors aware of your succession plan so they will not be shocked when it happens?
- ✓ Have you positioned your successor for success?

If you are a potential successor in an FOB,

- ✓ Are you sure you are? If not, can you find out and/or alter the outcome?
- ✓ Are you realistic about whether you are ready to take over—or truly want the responsibility?
- ✓ Are there other potential successors with whom you need to share thoughts?
- ✓ Is the founder dealing with realities, or do you need to take action to assure that the company is being protected during what could be a messy transition?
- ✓ Are you helping the founder consider posttransition options and offering appropriate assistance during the process and after?

Acknowledgments

This book would not be possible without the hard work and dedication of our many FOB team members who filled in for us and put up with us while we worked on it. Most especially, we appreciate the commitment of effort and generous spirit of Christine Ayala, who has hovered over every page in this book. Emiri Nakahara, Tashyna Wingo, Nicole Loucks, and James Trujillo have been essential to the process we've used to write a book together while running two different businesses. They epitomize what we speak of in this book regarding NFMs sharing family values and becoming trusted collaborators. They helped us write it with the freedom to be ourselves.

Special thanks to the excellent professional team at Greenleaf Book Group, led by Nathan True and Emilie Lyons; to Linda O'Doughda, our superb copy editor; and to Sheila Whalen and Bruce Wexler for editorial assistance. Every one of you helped this book evolve into what we hoped it would become.

We are truly grateful for our teams at Kolbe Corp and Dynamynd, Inc. who commit daily to the mission of our FOBs. They make everything we do possible—and joyful.

Thank you to the team at Strategic Coach for being a decades-long partner in reaching out to FOBs. Dan Sullivan, Babs Smith, and

Shannon Waller have proven to be the best of what business partners can be. We value their friendship.

A special thanks to our FMs about whom we write in *Business is Business*, David Kolbe and Will Rapp: *You deserve credit as the unnamed coauthors of many of the Dos and Don'ts of successfully working with family. Your wisdom is embedded in this book.*

A special thanks from Kathy: To Karen Kolbe—*Thanks for teaching me how a child can grow up in the midst of her mother's FOB and find the freedom to create her own highly successful business as a psychotherapist.*

A special thanks from Amy: To my husband, Jim, and our kids, CJ and Kate—*I am eternally grateful for your endless love and constant support that allow me to keep striving.*

Appendix

Following are details of the concepts and programs referenced throughout the book. This appendix includes the materials and programs we provide in seminars and consulting for families, founders, and family business employees.

**Kathy Kolbe's definition of success:
"Success is the freedom to be yourself."**

In order to be free to be yourself, you need to maximize the potential of all three of your mental factors.

Kolbe Theory of Conation

THREE MENTAL FACTORS/PARTS OF THE MIND

Ancient philosophers and modern psychologists share the concept of a three-part mind with separate domains for thinking, feeling, and doing. The conative or doing part contains the striving instincts that drive a person's natural way of taking action, or modus operandi (MO). This is the unique set of innate strengths and talents every person has that remain unchanged from birth. Everyone has an equal amount of conative energy for engaging the thinking (cognitive) and feeling (affective) parts of the mind to produce purposeful action.

Three Parts of the Mind

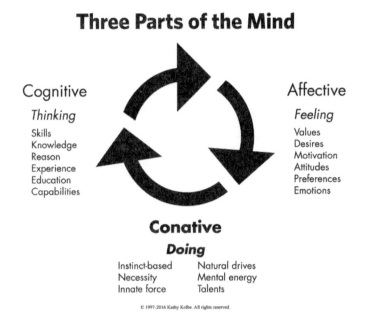

Cognitive

Thinking

Skills
Knowledge
Reason
Experience
Education
Capabilities

Affective

Feeling

Values
Desires
Motivation
Attitudes
Preferences
Emotions

Conative

Doing

Instinct-based	Natural drives
Necessity	Mental energy
Innate force	Talents

Conation

Conation is action derived from instinct; a purposeful mode of striving, volition. It is a conscious effort to carry out self-determined acts.

The Latin *conatus*, from which conation is derived, is defined as "any natural tendency, impulse, or directed effort."

Although ancient philosophers up through early 20th-century psychologists accepted conation, few concepts concerning it have survived unscathed from subsequent debates.

ACTION MODES

Kathy Kolbe was the first to identify four universal human instincts used in creative problem solving. These instincts are not measurable. The observable acts derived from them, however, can be identified and quantified by the Kolbe A™ Index (see Selected Kolbe Products and Services in the back of the book for more information). These instinct-driven behaviors are represented in the four Kolbe Action Modes: Fact Finder, Follow Thru, Quick Start, and Implementor.

THREE ZONES OF OPERATION IN THE FOUR ACTION MODES

There are three Zones of Operation in each of the four Action Modes measured on a unit scale of 1 to 10. Each utilizes equal amounts of mental energy for creative problem solving and decision making:

> **Initiating Actions:** The first thing people do is take actions that tie to their most insistent Action Mode. It's the longest line on their Kolbe A Index result. People will Initiate action through any of the Action Modes in which they have 7 to 10 units of conative energy (as shown on their Kolbe A Index result).
>
> **ReActions:** Conative ReActions moderate responses. They are an instinctive way of accommodating both Initiating actions and the natural push back to them, CounterActions. People ReAct in any mode in which they have 4 to 6 units of conative energy. ReActions are just as powerful as Initiating actions.
>
> **CounterActions:** Conative CounterActions offer a counterpoint to the way action is being taken; provide the instinctive strength to resist the way things are happening; and prevent problems when there is too much energy to Initiate a particular type of action. People CounterAct in any mode in which they have 1 to 3 units of conative energy. Like ReActions, CounterActions are just as powerful as Initiating actions.

Fact Finder: The instinctive way we gather and share information.

Behavior ranges from gathering detailed information and documenting strategies to simplifying and clarifying options.

OPERATING ZONE	FACT FINDER ACTIONS
Initiating	Details, strategies, research
ReActing	Specifics, editing, assessing pros and cons
CounterActing	Analysis paralysis, or minutiae

Follow Thru: The instinctive way we organize.

Behavior ranges from being systematic and structured to being adaptable and flexible.

OPERATING ZONE	FOLLOW THRU ACTIONS
Initiating	Systems, procedures, design, order
ReActing	Adjusting to existing plans, maintaining classifications
CounterActing	Getting boxed in, being overly structured

Quick Start: The instinctive way we deal with risk and uncertainty.

Behavior ranges from driving change and innovation to stabilizing and preventing chaos.

OPERATING ZONE	QUICK START ACTIONS
Initiating	Change, deadlines, uniqueness
ReActing	Mediating between the vision and the given
CounterActing	Chaos, a crisis atmosphere

Implementor: The instinctive way we handle space and tangibles.

Behavior ranges from making things more concrete by building solutions to being more abstract by imagining a solution.

OPERATING ZONE	IMPLEMENTOR ACTIONS
Initiating	Constructing, transporting, manipulating, and protecting tangible goods
ReActing	Using machinery or implements for either tangible or intangible effort
CounterActing	Need for tangible evidence or physical proof

Axioms in the Kolbe Theory of Conation

An axiom is a principle or truism on which an abstractly defined structure is based.

KOLBE AXIOMS RELATING TO INDIVIDUAL ACTIONS OR MOS

Axiom 1: Every human being has innate conative strengths.

Conative strengths are driven by universal instincts. They are observable as volitional or purposeful actions. These are controllable, intentional acts that surface from the unconscious level of instinct into the individual's awareness when there is motivation to strive toward conscious goals.

Axiom 2: Four Action Modes are universal methods of striving.

Every human being has a conative strength in each of four Action Modes used in problem solving. These are the basis of an individual's best methods of striving to reach a goal.

KOLBE ACTION MODE	STRIVING BEHAVIORS
Fact Finder	Gathering and sharing information
Follow Thru	Organizing
Quick Start	Dealing with risk and uncertainty
Implementor	Handling space and tangibles

Axiom 3: Conative strengths determine an individual's modus operandi, or MO. They are based upon how individuals operate in each Action Mode.

Conative strengths are quantifiable through the use of an algorithm that identifies an individual's natural way of operating (MO) through three Zones of Operation or ways of taking action in each of the four Action Modes.

These zones are measured on a 10-unit scale in results for conative assessments (the Kolbe A Index), enabling individuals to self-identify strengths within each Action Mode. These conative strengths are predictable and reliable.

Axiom 4: All human beings have equal but different conative strengths or natural abilities.

Each of the 12 conative strengths is of equal value in goal attainment or the creative problem-solving process. They are distributed equally between the genders and among the races. Because they are powered by instinct, they are embedded and consistent over an individual's lifetime. Therefore, an accurate measurement of conative strengths is unbiased by gender, race, and age.

12 Kolbe Strengths

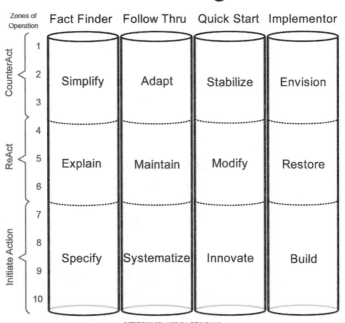

Zones of Operation	Fact Finder	Follow Thru	Quick Start	Implementor
CounterAct 1 2 3	Simplify	Adapt	Stabilize	Envision
ReAct 4 5 6	Explain	Maintain	Modify	Restore
Initiate Action 7 8 9 10	Specify	Systematize	Innovate	Build

© 1995-2016 Kathy Kolbe and Kolbe Corp. All Rights Reserved.

Conative strengths of parents, grandparents, and siblings do not predict an individual's MO. Therefore, it appears that conative strengths are not distributed genetically. Even identical twins have shown no greater probability of having similar MOs than has a random cross-section of the population.

Distribution on the scale of 1 to 10 in a randomly selected large population generally results in a bell-shaped or normal curve, indicating the measurement of a trait or characteristic of nature rather than nurture.

Axiom 5: Self-efficacy results from exercising control over personal conative strengths.

Self-awareness of conative strengths paves the way to exercising self-control over when and where to use those strengths. Persevering in their use provides a sense of self-efficacy. Conative strengths become observable during striving activities; otherwise, they are mere potential.

Axiom 6: Conative energy requires rejuvenation.

Instinctive energy that powers conative action is a finite resource, requiring rest and relaxation (the absence of striving) in order to be replenished.

Each unit of an individual's conative capacity can be considered an erg, with the full capacity being 100 ergs. Zones of Operation require different quantities of ergs.

Individuals tend to begin striving tasks by using the Action Mode for which they have the greatest number of ergs—even if instructions they receive tell them to do otherwise.

Axiom 7: Creativity requires use of all three mental factors.

All three parts of the mind contribute to the Kolbe Creative Process, which is synonymous with productivity. Each faculty operates independently, yet all three are equally important to the process.

A hierarchy of effort for all three faculties of the mind ties to the level of importance of the goals an individual seeks. This results in a hierarchy, or Dynamynd, of decision making. Success in reaching minor goals is necessary to prepare for success in reaching higher-level goals.

Other faculties of the mind may be impaired without diminishing the contribution of conative strengths. A disability in any faculty of the mind, however, will impact the creative process since it requires the integration of all three mental faculties.

KOLBE AXIOMS RELATING TO INTERACTIONS OR RELATIONSHIPS

Axiom 8: Conative stress results when obstacles interfere with the use of conative strengths.

Obstacles that interfere with an individual's free use of conative strengths limit the potential for success or goal attainment. Striving becomes less joyful and frustrations ensue.

Self-induced conative stress is caused by an individual attempting to work against his or her conative grain. It is like paddling a boat upstream. Much effort is made, with little progress to show for it.

Strain, or a depletion of mental energy, results from forcing efforts based on false self-expectations. It leads to mental burnout and low self-efficacy. This can be identified in the Kolbe Comparisons: A to B report.

When a number of people on a team are experiencing this strain, it has measurable negative results, which are identified and quantified in organizational reports by team strain.

Axiom 9: Significant differences in MOs between individuals create conative conflicts.

Differences in conative strengths between people can be of great benefit. People with significant differences in Kolbe Index results can fill in each other's gaps or collaborate by doing what the other won't do well. These differences can also be the source of relationship-damaging conflict, however, if either person considers the other's conative strengths to be a fault that needs fixing. This can be identified in the Comparisons: A to A report.

Axiom 10: Requirements that reduce a person's freedom to act on conative strengths diminish performance.

Attempts to force an individual to go against a conative grain causes tension and may escalate into the individuals acting out or shutting down.

Requirements that do not give individuals the freedom to use their conative strengths cause tension, which is a form of conative stress. This can be identified in the Comparisons: A to C report.

This happens with highly determined kids whose conative strengths are viewed as weaknesses. When their conative strengths are misidentified as ADD/ADHD, they suffer stress similar to that of workers who are told their conative strengths are inappropriate ways to perform job-related tasks.

In group settings, this diminished performance magnifies and results in a higher probability of team tension.

KOLBE AXIOMS RELATING TO INTERACTIONS OR GROUP BEHAVIORS

Axiom 11: Synergy is a quantifiable conative factor.

Synergy comes from the right combination of MOs in a group of collaborators. A group that collectively has every zone in each mode will have all the conative talents in its arsenal. An ideal group would reflect the Zones of Operation as they naturally occur in the population, with 25 percent of their conative strengths Initiating solutions in any mode, 50 percent accommodating, and 25 percent preventing problems. A strategic balance of MOs in a group of collaborators increases the probability of goal attainment.

Degrees of conative Synergy are predicted by the distribution of 12 conative strengths among team members.

Axiom 12: Conative Cloning is caused by redundant conative strengths.

A group with Conative Cloning, or too much energy in one zone of an Action Mode, will show symptoms of inertia and become plagued with inaction; no forward action; or a narrow, repetitive approach to problem solving. The group has essentially cloned itself and often finds false comfort in their sameness (birds of a feather flock together), failing to find the benefits of Synergistic conative talents.

Axiom 13: Polarization results when opposite conative strengths pull against each other.

Polarization is often present in groups in which participants fight among themselves. When conative talents for an Action Mode within a group are at opposite ends of the scale, actions become unproductive as each polar set of talents conflicts without enough accommodating energy. The problem-solving methods are so far apart that consensus building is difficult.

Axiom 14: Probability of team success improves as conative strengths are appropriately allocated.

Having the right people doing the right jobs is a matter of having the right conative fit. Assigning people to tasks for which they have the wrong conative strengths robs them and the organization of their opportunity to succeed.

High productivity is predicted in organizations with a high percentage of people who are able to contribute their conative strengths. As conative stress or the inability to contribute conative strengths increases among people in an organization, so do absenteeism, turnover, dissatisfaction, and errors.

Use of time and energy

Everyone runs out of time and energy. You can't get time back—once it's used, it's gone—but energy *can* be renewed with rest and relaxation (the absence of striving). Everyone has an equal amount of conative energy (100 units of instinctive power) measured in ergs. An individual's 100 ergs of mental energy are equal to the energy available to every other human being. Each of your 100 ergs has the same intensity, whether it is in the Initiating, ReActing, or CounterActing zone.

Zones of Operation require different quantities of ergs: The greater your numerical result in a particular Action Mode, the more ergs you have driving the use of that Action Mode. As we mentioned earlier, individuals begin striving tasks by using the Action Mode in which they have the greatest number of ergs despite the instructions to do otherwise.

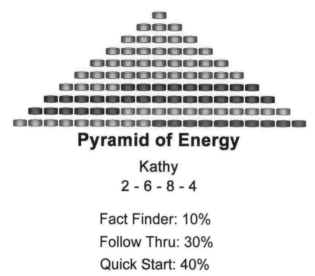

Pyramid of Energy

Kathy
2 - 6 - 8 - 4

Fact Finder: 10%
Follow Thru: 30%
Quick Start: 40%
Implementor: 20%

Use of time by Action Mode

- **Fact Finder:** Gauges how much time something will take through experience and expertise; puts events into a historical perspective.

- **Follow Thru:** Sequences events and provides continuity, paces oneself; sets a rhythm for effort and coordinates with others.

- **Quick Start:** Predicts and deals with events ahead of time; focuses on future by forecasting what could be, anticipates change.

- **Implementor:** Grounded in the here and now, wanting the moment to last; creates quality products that will endure through time.

The Dynamynd Decision Ladder

The Dynamynd is a model of the emotions, thoughts, and actions involved when making different levels of decision. It clarifies the need to go beyond simply having these amazing attributes and will coach you on maximizing your use of them. Your self-fulfillment and contribution to society can be tracked by assessing the levels you achieve in each of these aspects of your mental makeup.

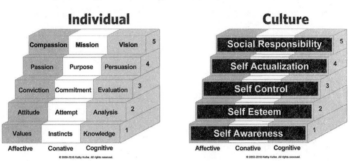

Kinds of effort

- **Efforts:** Conative actions you take to solve problems.

- **Best efforts:** Action that uses your MO or instinctive abilities.

- **Foolish efforts:** Actions you take that you know are not your best efforts.

- **Wasted efforts:** Energy you use to take action that goes against your grain, or is contrary to your best efforts.

Kathy Kolbe's 5 Rules for Trusting Your Instincts

1. **Act—Before You Think.** Do what you never thought you could.

When you Act—Before You Think, it keeps you from rationalizing your way out of making a decision. Don't stop and consider what you should do; instead, trust your instincts. Too often people fear looking foolish and, as a result, end up being victims. They don't run out of the church when their gut tells them not to say, "I do." Or they don't run for cover before disaster strikes.

2. **Self-Provoke**. Get where you want to go.

Goad yourself to Initiate the action you desire. Some ways to self-provoke are below

- Inspire your own achievements.
- Direct your energies.
- Push yourself into action.
- Make what you want to happen, happen.
- Ignite your own instincts.
- Create your own opportunities.

3. **Commit—But to Very Little.** Target your top priorities.

You need to make commitments, but if you commit to too many things at one time, your instincts will get whiplash. They'll be thrust back and forth among so many priorities that you'll find it difficult to concentrate on what matters most.

We recommend commitment contracts between people, both at work and at home. It's a process that lays out the use of time and mental energy so both parties can see the logic of how they're allocated. It brings reality into conversations that can become strictly emotional and accusatory.

4. **Be Obstinate—in Overcoming Obstacles**. Stick with your instincts.

Being obstinate includes tenacity, perseverance, and dogged resolution, having a ruling passion, being willful, and acting with determination.

If you don't overcome the obstacles that keep you from having the freedom to act on instinct, you will never live up to your potential.

5. **Do Nothing—When Nothing Works.** Take charge of time-outs.

This is how you protect the use of your instinctive energy. It helps you shut off the energy leaks that go toward nonpurposeful actions. It removes the mental clutter in your life.

Research

STUDY ON BIAS AND THE KOLBE INSTRUMENT

Dr. Robert T. Keim of the Decision Systems Research Center of Arizona State University conducted an extensive study on bias and the Kolbe instrument in 1990, in which he examined 4030 Kolbe results which were broken down into 17 groups reflecting common conative patterns similar to job selection criteria.

Evaluation of the intensities by Action Mode for a group of 1447 males and 1125 females who took the Kolbe Index in Kathy Kolbe's book *The Conative Connection* revealed remarkably similar distributions.

Intensities by Action Mode

Gender	Mode	Mean Score	Std Deviation
Male	FF	6.164	.372
Female		6.136	.344
Male	FT	3.665	1.071
Female		3.621	1.074
Male	QS	7.547	.625
Female		7.575	.607
Male	IM	2.882	.896
Female		2.917	.925

The Statistical Handbook © 2009 All Rights Reserved by Kolbe Corp

The results again support that neither gender is more likely to follow a particular pattern of scores. The frequency table is presented below.

Frequency of Distribution in Action Modes and Zones of Operation

Mode	Gender	% Initiate	% Accommodate	% Resist
FF	Male	34.14	53.28	12.58
	Female	33.60	52.80	13.60
FT	Male	19.56	51.69	28.75
	Female	22.22	53.33	24.44
QS	Male	38.77	32.07	29.16
	Female	40.71	33.78	25.51
IM	Male	12.23	48.86	38.91
	Female	8.36	47.38	44.27
Total	Male	26.17	46.48	27.35
	Female	26.22	46.82	26.96

The Statistical Handbook © 2009 All Rights Reserved by Kolbe Corp

TEST–RETEST RELIABILITY STUDY

A study was completed to assess the test–retest reliability of Kolbe A Index scores of 282 participants who had taken the Kolbe A Index at different times prior to July 2006. Subjects were contacted via email to request that they participate in a retest of the Index. Participation in the retest was voluntary, but most of the respondents took the initial Kolbe A Index as part of their employment. The retest data were gathered by the Center for Conative Abilities between March and July of 2006.

Frequency Distribution of
Zone Scores and Percentages of Change

Time 1 Years (n)	Absolute value of zone change	Number (Percentage) of participants whose scores reflect a zone change			
		Fact Finder	Follow Thru	Quick Start	Implementor
1991-2006 (*n*=282)	0	201 (71.3)	189 (67.0)	199 (70.6)	208 (73.8)
	1	81 (28.7)	93 (33.0)	80 (28.4)	72 (25.5)
	2	0 (0)	0 (0)	3 (1.1)	2 (.7)
1991-1995 (*n*=64)	0	43 (67.2)	42 (65.6)	45 (70.3)	43 (67.2)
	1	21 (32.8)	22 (34.4)	17 (26.6)	21 (23.8)
	2	0 (0)	0 (0)	2 (3.1)	0 (0)
1996-1998 (*n*=55)	0	38 (69.1)	36 (65.5)	38 (69.1)	40 (72.7)
	1	17 (30.9)	19 (34.5)	17 (30.9)	14 (25.5)
	2	0 (0)	0 (0)	0 (0)	1 (1.8)
1999-2001 (*n*=51)	0	38 (74.5)	33 (64.7)	40 (78.4)	42 (82.4)
	1	13 (25.5)	18 (35.3)	11 (21.6)	9 (17.6)
	2	0 (0)	0 (0)	0 (0)	0 (0)
2002-2004* (*n*=60)	0	47 (78.3)	43 (71.7)	41 (68.3)	41 (68.3)
	1	13 (21.7)	17 (28.3)	18 (30)	19 (31.7)
	2	0 (0)	0 (0)	1 (1.7)	0 (0)
2005-2006* (*n*=52)	0	35 (67.3)	35 (67.3)	35 (67.3)	42 (80.8)
	1	1 (32.7)	17 (32.7)	17 (32.7)	9 (17.3)
	2	0 (0)	0 (0)	0 (0)	1 (1.9)

*Sub-sample reflects 2002 revision of some questions impacting the Implementor score

OTHER KOLBE RESEARCH

For more information on Kolbe research studies including Validity, Reliability, and many others, please visit www.kolbe.com/research.

**For information about using
Kolbe Wisdom in your business:**

www.kolbe.com

602-840-9770

info@kolbe.com

Glossary

These terms are defined as used by Kathy Kolbe in her Theory of Conation.

Accommodate—See ReAct.

Action Modes—As identified by Kathy Kolbe, four distinct clusters of measurable behavior that result from engaging our striving instincts: Fact Finder, Follow Thru, Quick Start, and Implementor.

Affect/affective—Known for centuries as one of the three parts of the mind. Pertains to or arises from feelings or emotions as measured on personality or social style instruments. An emotion or tendency.

CoAct—Initiating action in a Kolbe Action Mode combined with another insistent (or highly responding) mode. The Initiating actions will have a duality of expression in those two modes. Formerly referred to as *Natural Advantages*.

Cognition/cognitive—Known for centuries as one of the three parts of the mind. Deals with knowledge, competencies, and intellectual processes as measured on IQ or skills tests.

Commitment—Guarantee that the necessary instinctive power will be allocated to accomplish a goal.

Conation/conative—Known for centuries as one of the three parts of the mind. Actions derived from instinct; related to striving and volition. Can be measured by the Kolbe A Index.

Conative Cloning—Replication of Kolbe Strengths; too much of a good a thing.

Conative stress—The result of a compelling need being denied when one's natural drive is thwarted, creating unproductive pressure on the individual.

Conflict—As defined by Kathy Kolbe, conative stress that results from natural differences of four units or more in how people function in any one Action Mode.

CounterAct—The instinctive way of resisting certain activities in an Action Mode as a unique method of problem solving. A measurement of 1–3 units of mental energy in an Action Mode. Also known as *prevent* or *resist*.

Creative process—See *Kolbe Creative Process.*

Dynamynd Decision Ladder—A hierarchical model of the graduated, sequential steps that lead to higher levels of thinking, feeling, and taking action in the creative problem-solving process.

Levels of effort—The degree to which we decide to employ our mental energy or engage our instincts as represented on a scale. (See *will.*) Lowest level—intention; middle level—attempt; highest level—commitment.

Erg—Smallest single unit of energy.

Facilitator—A person with three or four Action Modes in the mid-range and no mode of Initiating action. Also termed *Mediator.*

Fact Finder—The instinctive way we gather and share information. Behavior ranges from striving to be a specialist by gathering detailed information to someone who will naturally simplify by generalizing.

FM—Abbreviation for family member.

FOB—Abbreviation for family-owned business.

Follow Thru—The instinctive way we organize. Behavior ranges from being systematic and structured to someone who will be more adaptable by varying the approach.

Implementor—The instinctive way we handle space and tangibles. Behavior ranges from making things more concrete by building solutions to someone who will be more abstract by imagining a solution.

Inertia—Loss of productivity caused by uniformity of action among people in an organization. Also known as *Conative Cloning*.

Initiate—How an individual starts the problem-solving process. The instinctive way of approaching a solution to a problem through any Action Mode. A measurement of 7–10 units of conative energy in any Action Mode. Also referred to as *insistence*.

Instinct—Occurring below the conscious level, a natural or inherent impulse resulting in a pattern of behaviors.

Kolbe Creative Process—The mental process that results in the development of something that has not previously existed; also the mental process that naturally takes place when the mind is focused on solving a particular problem.

Kolbe Strengths—The 12 ways of taking instinctive action when problem solving. Each of us takes action in each of the four Action Modes and our uniqueness derives from the combinations.

Kolbe Theory of Conation—The theory of individual performance driven by instinctive behaviors originated by Kathy Kolbe. It includes psychometric measurements identifying natural talents and providing a pathway to higher productivity and greater satisfaction. Details of the Theory are described in the Kolbe Axioms (see page 211).

Mental energy—Internal power sources available to drive one's instincts toward goal-directed activity.

MO/method of operation/modus operandi—A numerical representation of one's instinctive way of taking action as measured across the four Kolbe Action Modes.

Natural advantage—See *CoAct*.

NFM—Abbreviation for non–family member.

Prevent—See *CounterAct*. Also known as resistance.

Quick Start—The instinctive way we deal with risk and uncertainty. Behavior ranges from driving change and innovation to someone who will stabilize by preventing chaos.

ReAct—A mid-range positioning of 4–6 units in a given Action Mode describing the ability to bridge differences between those on the outermost limits who Initiate solutions or prevent problems in the same Action Mode.

Strain—As defined by Kathy Kolbe, conative stress resulting from a person's unrealistic self-expectations of how he or she needs to perform.

Striving Instincts—Mental energies that are universal, intrinsic, individual talents, seminal, valid across cultures, needs, innate, natural, authentic and inborn tendencies to strive or Initiate action through probing, patterning, innovating, and demonstrating. See also *Instinct*.

Synergy—Kathy Kolbe defines Synergy as a productive balance of complementary conative talents. The ideal distribution of conative energy is 25 percent CounterActing problems, 50 percent ReActing to problems, and 25 percent Initiating solutions.

Tension—As defined by Kathy Kolbe, conative stress resulting from another person's unrealistic requirements for how a person will perform.

Will—The power of control the mind has over whether, or to what degree, to engage the striving instincts. Although an intellectual awareness of the need to employ these instincts or an affective concern for their use may exist, free will makes that determination.

Zones of Operation—The perspective through which people naturally use a Striving Instinct—what they will do, won't do, or are willing to do. In Kathy Kolbe's expression, the zones include Initiate (insistence), CounterAct (prevention or resistance), and ReAct (response or accommodation).

Selected Kolbe Products and Services for Family Businesses

Professional Services

Kolbe TeamSuccess Seminar for Family Businesses—A dynamic full- or half-day session that provides an interactive way to explore the workings of specific teams within a family business. The seminar inventories instinctive talents that make up the actual—not just desired—culture. Participants learn ways to leverage these strengths, enabling FMs and NFMs to work together consistently and effectively. Leaders are given diagnostic and prescriptive information to accelerate team productivity as well as tools to improve communication and clarify commitment levels.

Kolbe Leadership Training—A one-day course to develop current and next-generation leaders by giving them the tools to improve performance, increase retention, and boost the engagement of the company's most valuable asset—its employees.

Coaching for FOB Leaders—Customized one-on-one or group sessions with a Kolbe Certified Master Consultant designed to analyze strategic challenges, manage interpersonal conflicts, and harmonize individual talents with family business goals.

Kolbe Certification—An immersive three-day seminar that provides organizational leaders and management consultants with an in-depth understanding of the Kolbe System and foundational theory. This highly interactive training experience provides participants with the tools and knowledge to become in-house or independent Kolbe Certified Consultants. Kolbe Certification also includes training on how to generate and interpret Kolbe WAREwithal online management reports.

Kolbe Indexes

The Kolbe A Index is a 36-question instrument designed to measure the conative faculty of the mind—the instinctive talents that drive the way a person takes action. The result, called the *modus operandi* (MO), is the innate method of operation that enables an individual to be productive. Research on the Kolbe A Index indicates no significant differences in outcome by age, race, gender, or physical handicap.

Kolbe B Index is a 24-question instrument that measures the functional demands of your current position. The results help you understand which of your talents will be a natural fit for the job and how you, as the jobholder, view the requirements for success in the role.

Kolbe C Index is a 24-question instrument that measures the functional expectations of a specific position. The results help identify how the evaluator believes the job needs to be done for the jobholder to be successful in the position. This unique job assessment tool helps you target the methods of operation that underlie success in the role. These are the ways the jobholder needs to take action, regardless of skills, intelligence, or personality. Where multiple people do the same role, one Kolbe C may be sufficient.

Kolbe Y Index is an assessment similar to the Kolbe A Index but designed for young people with a 4th through 11th grade reading level. Online results include an audio recording explaining how a young person can use his or her instinctive capabilities to create effective solutions to problems.

Parent Guide is an easy-to-follow online resource that aids parents and caregivers in supporting their child's striving instincts. Parents learn how to recognize and honor their child's instinctive strengths so they can provide support with solving problems, improving communication skills, and increasing the opportunity for personal success in school, extracurricular activities, social situations, and at home.

Kolbe R Index is a 36-question assessment that measures one person's expectations of his or her spouse, parent, sibling, or other person in a personal relationship.

Powerful solutions for family businesses

Kolbe Coaching Reports: Detail the best ways to manage and motivate someone by tapping into his or her instinctive talents. Designed specially for managers and supervisors, each four-page report is customized for a specific person's Kolbe A Index result and offers individualized strategies for improving performance.

Comparisons—A to A: Provides an analysis of conative strengths and potential for conative stress between two individuals with a customized report prepared for each of them. Includes Conables tips designed just for you to increase productivity and meaningful communication.

Comparisons—A to B: Analyzes how a person's instinctive strengths (Kolbe A Index result) compare to his or her self-expectations of the job (Kolbe B result) and provides strategies to increase productivity and reduce stress.

Comparisons—A to C: Analyzes how a person's instinctive strengths (Kolbe A Index result) compare to his or her job, as described by anyone in a position to evaluate the role (Kolbe C result) and provides strategies to increase efficiency and reduce stress.

Commitment Clarifier: An easy-to-use worksheet and leader's guide that creates a process for fulfilling work and personal obligations. By analyzing tasks from the perspective of all three parts of the mind, the Commitment Clarifier helps busy professionals prioritize tasks, delegate specific responsibilities, and establish clear goals.

Kolbe Bottom Lines booklet: A pocket-sized reference guide to key concepts of the Kolbe System for use in understanding, interpreting, and comparing Kolbe Index results.

Leadership Analytics (LEAN): Solutions apply the latest breakthroughs in Kolbe Wisdom to organizational challenges and provide customized, ready-to-implement solutions for leaders and managers. By assessing the factors that determine a team's success, LEAN helps identify not just the cause of team productivity and efficiency problems but also the corrective strategies to solve them.

Team Collaboration Survey: A free survey that will quickly determne whether a team functions more collaborativly or more independently. It offers customized Leadership Tips designed to boost productivity immediately. teamsurvey.kolbe.com/bib

Kolbe RightFit Hiring System: Kolbe Corp's statistically proven hiring tool that helps companies screen and select the best job applicants. Instead of guessing how well a prospective employee will perform, RightFit helps you identify the required instinctive methods of operation, or profile, of the ideal candidate.

The Dynamynd Interview: Provides a step-by-step process for discovering whether a candidate exhibits the level of effort you need for a specific position. It provides interview questions, advice on how to interpret answers, and worksheets to keep track of interviewees' responses.

Apt Careers: A quantum leap in career discovery, Apt rates 1,200+ careers with the likelihood for success just for YOU. Unlike other career assessments, it provides career opportunities that align with individual's natural talents while highlighting great careers outside of your interest areas and listing careers that will cause you stress in the long term. Based on decades of research on the instinctive strengths that managers reward in the workplace, Apt's seven-minute survey will provide careers that offer you the freedom to be yourself!

Takes Two: Compares a couple's conative differences and uncovers the hidden factors that help—or hurt—your committed romantic relationship.

Book Kathy Kolbe or Amy Burske to speak at your event

Both Kolbe and Bruske are dynamic, sought-after speakers who enjoy working with new and diverse audiences. They will inspire, inform and engage with direct and timely messages that embolden people to do what they do best. Whether it's a keynote presentation, industry workshop, or executive retreat, they deliver unique insight with a lasting impact for all who attend.

Please contact
info@businessisbusinessbook.com for more information.

Also available from Kathy Kolbe

Wisdom of the Ages
Think-ercise! books and games:

- How to Raise a Gifted Child
- Do It Yourself Critical and Creative Thinking
- Ouchless Curiosity
- Joy of Learning
- . . . and 68 additional Think-ercise books and games for K–12 students

**For more information on Kolbe
Solutions for family-owned businesses:**

www.kolbe.com

602-840-9770

info@kolbe.com

Index

Note: Page numbers in **bold** indicate the definition of the topic.

A

AAD (Arrogant Attitude Disorder), 145

Accommodation in an Action Mode, 48

Action Modes
overview, **225**
Continuum of Behavior, 13–14
CounterActions, 16, 46–47, 164, 179
effects of imbalance on team Synergy, 162–65
Initiating Action, 44–46
Initiating needs in transitions, 178
ReActions, 17–18, 48, **228**
research, 221–22
Zones of Operation, 15–18, 221–22
See also personal brand by Action Mode; *entries beginning with* Quick Start behavior

Action Modes behaviors
Fact Finder, 14, 16, 45, 46, 56, **227**
Fact Finder CounterActors, 56, 94, 200

Fact Finder Initiators, 79–81, 93–94, 118–19, 150, 163, 200
Fact Finder Researcher, 45
Follow Thru, 14, 15, 45, 56, 57, **227**
Follow Thru CounterActors, 94
Follow Thru Initiator CounterActors, 118
Follow Thru Initiators, 56, 81, 94, 118, 150–51, 163, 177–78
Follow Thru Organizer, 45
Implementor, 14, 17–18, 46, 47, **227**
Implementor CounterActors, 94
Implementor Initiators, 81, 94, 118, 151, 164
Implementor Protector, 46
Implementor Quick Start Initiation, 142–43
Quick Start CounterActors, 79, 94, 177–78
Quick Start Initiators, 79, 81, 94, 151, 163, 178, 194, 200
Quick Start Innovators, 45
Quick Start ReActions, 200
See also Quick Start behavior
adaptable Follow Thru person, 47

affect/affective part of the mind
    overview, 9, 12, **225**
    affective therapy vs. conative con-
        sulting, 115–17
    and competing commitments,
        31–33
    desire to help as, 115
ambition. *See* next-generation ambi-
    tion development
Apt Careers online program, 115–16,
    148, 235
arrogance vs. confidence, 144–46
Arrogant Attitude Disorder (AAD),
    145
attempt vs. best possible effort, 38–39

B

birth order myths, 132–33
Bottom Lines booklet, 234
boundaries, 73–90
    overview, 73–74
    avoiding unnecessary barriers
        between FMs and NFMs,
        87–89
    avoiding "us and them" cliques
        within the FOB, 89–90, 91
    and establishment of roles, 104
    flexible boundary benefits and
        risks, 74–76
    leaving FM work relationships at
        work, 76–77
    pre-FOB contracts for spouses,
        77–81
    protecting access to intellectual
        property, 85–86
    recognizing conflicts between fam-
        ily and business loyalty, 84–85
    separation of business and home
        life, 76
    and sibling rivalries, 81–84
    space and equipment boundaries,
        86–87

on stage vs. backstage, 100–01
Bruske, Amy (coauthor/daughter)
    advisory board evaluation of,
        25–26
    joining Kolbe Corp, 82–84
    Kathy questions Amy's pizza order
        for staff meeting, 195–96
    mentoring relationship with Kathy,
        124–27
    transition from Kathy as CEO
        to David and Amy in charge,
        199–202
business values vs. family values,
    27–28

C

career assessment, Apt Careers,
    115–16, 148, 235
career choice and conative instincts,
    115–16
certification. *See* Kolbe Certification
charisma, 93–94
children. *See* next-generation ambi-
    tion development
choice making skill development,
    146–47
cliques, 89–90
closed space for groups, 165–66
Coaching for FOB Leaders, 232
Coaching Reports, 233
CoAct, **225**
cognition/cognitive part of the mind
    overview, **225**
    as ability to do a job, 115
    contributions of employees, 10–12
    and marriage partners, 59
Collaborative Teams, 9, 156, 157,
    160–165
collaborators vs. cliques, 89–90
commitment, **226**
    attempt vs., 38–39

balancing empathy for an FM and, 135–36

competing commitments of business, 31–33

FMs commitment level, 40–41

Commitment Clarifier, 234

communication, 91–107

overview, 91

with actions, 106–07

bringing up business issue in family situations, 95–96

direct vs. manipulative techniques, 104–06

empowering, intriguing, and inspiring the next generation, 142–43

establishing guidelines for discussing business on personal time, 96–98

FOB style and culture, 92–93, 122–23

and nonverbal communication, 99–100

on social media, 101–02

on stage vs. backstage demeanor, 100–02

as transparent, honest, and realistic, 103–04

use first names at the business, not family titles or nicknames, 98–99

utilizing the best means for, 102–03

Comparisons—A to A report, 125–26, 135, 234

Comparisons—A to B report, 234

Comparisons—A to C report, 234

compensation considerations, 167–70

conation/conative part of the mind, **226**

overview, 9, 12–14, 208

danger of guessing, 134–35

conative consulting vs. affective therapy, 115–17

conative strengths, 48–50, 144–46

maximizing conative strengths, 48–50

and MOs, 118–19

and outlook on transitions, 177–81

and risk taking, 79

and transitions, 177–81

Conative Cloning/inertia, 163–64, 216, **226**, 227

conative conflicts, **84**

conative effort, 41–43, 109–10. *See also* communication

conative instincts and career choice, 115–16

conative research, 133

conative stress, 141, **226**

confidence vs. arrogance, 144–46

conflict

overview, **226**

conative, 84

loyalty issues, 84–85

outside advisors as facilitators, 89–90

consultants for transition orchestration, 181–82

Continuum of Behavior in Action Modes, 14

corporate secrets/intellectual property, 67, 85–86

CounterAct/CounterActions

examples, **16**

in problem-solving process, 46–47

and transitions, 179

tug-of-war with Initiators, 164

couples

betrayal by, 68–69

on different sides of labor and management, 84–85

discussing work at home, 96–97

guessing conative strengths of
partner, 135
power struggles, 80
pre-FOB contracts and ground
rules for working together,
77–81
Takes Two program, 235
and trust, 59
creative problem solving, 139, 142,
148–49
creative process, **226**
crisis management, 61–63

D

decision making, 146–47, 173–74.
See also Action Modes
direct communication, 104–06
disciplinary discussions with FMs, 97
discrimination and values, 30
Do Nothing—when Nothing Works,
36, 50–51, 184
Dos and *Don'ts*. *See* guidelines
(*Don'ts*); guidelines (*Dos*)
dreams
of FOB founder, 32–33
of parents for their children, 11–12
Dynamynd Decision Ladder, 219,
226
Dynamynd Interview process, 37, 235

E

effort, 35–52
overview, 35–36
attempt vs. best possible effort,
38–39
doing what matters most, including nothing, 50–51
mental energy management, 41–43
price of high productivity, 36–38
rewards for, 39–41
See also personal brand by Action
Mode
email for communicating, 102–03

empathy for another FM, 135–36
employees
combinations that create Synergy,
160–65
imposing personal values on,
29–31
key influencers, 181–82
objective criteria for hiring,
134–35
pay levels, 39
recognition and compensation
considerations, 167–70
See also FMs; non–family members
entitlement, avoiding feelings of,
122–23
ergs, 41–43, 48–49, **226**
ethical issues specific to FOBs, 65–67
examples and stories
allowing sink or swim moments,
128–29
allowing unproductive FM to be
laid off, 129–30
board of advisors asserting wrong
values, 25–27
child's freedom to develop MO,
142–44
communication with children, 142
consistent application of values,
28–29
couple discussing work at home,
96–97
couple on different sides of labor
and management, 84–85
delegation of duties, 104
destruction of business, 183,
184–85
father's ability to teach vs. son's
willingness to initiate, 113
FM/FOB conative mismatch,
9–12, 15–18
FMs bringing work home, 95–96
FM's vs. NFM's personal hard-
ships, 168
FOB founder and his daughter's
separate objectives, 32–33

FOB in trouble "grabbed" by competent leader, 194
FOB with competing commitments, 31–32
founder trusts instincts of others more than his own, 56–57
gender bias and birth order myths, 132–33
hiring the right NFM, 37–38
humility, 145–46
independent work by team members, 166–67
indirect communication, 104–06
instilling confidence, 149
Kolbe Corp
laying off a FM, 187–88
mental energy based on job satisfaction, 41–43
mentoring relationship development, 124–27
morale issues at multilevel marketing company, 169–70
NFM empowerment, 63–64
NFMs/FMs—appropriate boundaries, 87–89
parent wants payback for daughter's training, 114–15
power struggles, 185–86
professional firm integrates FM slowly, 121–22
prospective CEO daughter fails to implement FOB values, 176–77
setting the tone with first names, 98–99
siblings as coworking FMs, 82–84
siblings playing and working together, 156
theft by FMs, 62, 68
thinking-based issue, 11
too many Fact Finders create stagnation, 162, 163
unmotivated son joins the FOB, 23–25

expectations, 59–61, 82, 121–22

F

face-to-face meetings for communicating, 103
Facilitators, **226**
Fact Finder behavior, 14, 16, 45, 46, 56, **227**
Fact Finder CounterActors, 56, 94, 200
Fact Finder Initiators, 79–81, 93–94, 118–19, 150, 163, 200
Fact Finder Researcher, 45
failure
    allowing FMs' failure, 127–29
    and family security, 8
    mistakes vs. unethical behavior, 69
    sharing yours with FMs, 127
false expectations, 59–61, 82
family life sacrifices, 119–20, 141–42
family members. *See* FMs
family-owned businesses (FOBs)
    overview, 2–4, 7–8
    as career vs. job, 40–41
    ethical issues specific to, 65–67
    global productivity, 36
    job security in, 186–87
    leaving work relationship at work, 76–77
    principles for success, 4–5
    professionalism in the workplace, 98–100
    style and culture, 92–93, 122–23, 182
    support persons for FMs, 49–50
    and trusting your instincts, 54–55
family values vs. business values, 27–28
fear of betrayal, 65–66
flexible boundaries, 74–76
FM development, 109–37
    overview, 109
    and Conative MOs, 118–19

family life sacrifices lead to FOB
    resentment, 119–20
finding their niche, 109–10
freedom to be yourself as priority,
    112–14
jobs for FMs who aren't interested
    but need work, 120
matching interests and natural
    abilities, 114–17
preventing problems when off-
    spring join the FOB, 111–12
FMs (family members)
    betrayal by FM, 66–69
    betrayal by FOB, 65
    building on strengths, 9–14
    commitment level, 40–41
    empathy for, 135–36
    FM/FOB personality mismatch
        example, 9–12, 15–18
    form for communication with
        NFMs, 103
    guidelines for discussing business
        on personal time, 96–98
    and NFM coworkers, 64–65,
        86–87
    NFM integration with, 27–28,
        87–89
    office/space locations, 165–66
    opportunities to achieve full poten-
        tial, 127–29
    resentment of family's sacrifices,
        119–20
    terminating a FM, 187–90
    and trust, 53, 58–59
    value-added requirement, 8–9,
        23–25, 123–24
    values assessment, 27–28
    values of, 22–25
    See also couples; parents; role place-
        ment of FMs
FOBs. See family-owned businesses
Follow Thru behavior, 14, 15, 45, 47,
    56, **227**

Follow Thru CounterActors, 94
Follow Thru Initiator CounterActors,
    118
Follow Thru Initiators, 56, 81, 94,
    118, 150–51, 163, 177–78
Follow Thru Organizer, 45
founders, 196–97, 199–202. See also
    leadership
fuzzy logic, 73

G

gender bias, 132–33
golden rule: trust your instincts,
    53–54
graceful exits
    overview, 193–95
    of founders and FOB leaders,
        196–97
    moving forward, 199–202
    Reality Check, 203
    seeing humor in the process of
        "letting go," 195–96
    ugly exit prevention, 197–99
guidelines (Don'ts)
    accept the "I dunno" response,
        146–47
    act on gender biases or birth order
        myths, 132–33
    bring FM work relationships
        home, 76–77
    bring up business issue in family
        situations, 95–96
    don't use others to manipulate
        FMs, 104–06
    give a job to FMs just because they
        need work, 23–25, 120
    for graceful exits, 198–99
    hide the realities of work from
        future FMs, 152–53
    for laying off an FM, 190
    limit FM interns to a narrow group
        of jobs, 152

for orchestrating transitions, 189–90

to prevent problems when off-spring join the FOB, 111–12

protect FMs from failure, 127–29

put FMs on a pedestal, 129–30

for social media arena, 101–02

for teams, 159

use NFMs as "babysitters," 130–32

guidelines (*Dos*)

address FMs in the business by first names, not family titles or nicknames, 98–99

allow unproductive FM to be laid off, 129–30

anticipate sibling rivalries, 81–84

avoid feeding feelings of entitlement, 122–23

avoid unnecessary barriers between FMs and NFMs, 87–89

avoid "us and them" cliques within the FOB, 89–90, 91

be aware of your nonverbal communication, 99–100

be clear about on stage vs. backstage demeanor, 100–02

communicate directly, 104–06

communicate with transparency and honesty, but be realistic, 103–04

consider pre-FOB contracts for spouses, 77–81

develop confidence, not arrogance, 144–46

establish guidelines for discussing business on personal time, 96–98

for teams, 159

give FMs opportunities to achieve full potential, 127–29

for graceful exits, 198–99

have realistic expectations, 121–22

help kids play to their strengths, 147–48

include the next gen in professional growth opportunities, 149–51

know when to email, phone, or meet face-to-face, 102–03

laying off an FM, 189–90

let FMs experience the realities of work, 152–53

let FMs learn from your mistakes, 127

listen to future FMs, 148–49

match mentors by MOs, 124–27

for orchestrating transitions, 189–90

protect access to intellectual property, 85–86

recognize conflicts between family and business loyalty, 84–85

require FMs to gain experience elsewhere first, 123–24

rules for trusting your instincts, 220–21

set space and equipment boundaries, 86–87

for teams, 159

use the same objective criteria for hiring FMs and NFMs, 134–35

gut check, 55–57

H

"helicopter" FOB founders, 127

human productivity
overview, 5
affective factors, 9, 12
building on strengths, 9–14
cognitive factors, 9, 10–12
conative factors, 9, 12–14, 13–17
price for, 36–38
See also next-generation ambition development

humility, learning, 145–46

Hybrid Team, 100–01, **157**–60, 165, 168

I

Ideal Synergistic team, 162
"I dunno" response, 146–47
Implementor behavior, 14, 17–18, 46, 47, **227**
Implementor CounterActors, 94
Implementor Initiators, 81, 94, 118, 151, 164
Implementor Protector, 46
Implementor Quick Start initiatives, 142–43
indecisiveness, 146–47
Independent Team, 156–158, 166–67
Indexes, 143, 232–33. *See also* Kolbe A Index
inertia/Conative Cloning, 163–64, 216, 226, **227**
Initator tug of war with CounterActors, 164
Initiate, **227**
Initiating Action, 44–46
Innovators. *See* Quick Start behavior
instincts
    overview, 53–54, **227**
    of FMs, 58–59
    instinct-based natural drives, 55–57, 144
    trusting instincts of others, 60–61
    trusting your own, 51, 53–55, 220–21
intellectual property/corporate secrets, 67, 85–86
interactive team. *See* Collaborative Team
IQ and cognitive skills, 11

K

key influencers, 181–82
Kolbe, David (son), 25–26, 82–84, 199–202
Kolbe, Kathy
    discussing work at home, 97–98
    and Kolbe Corp, 7–8
    leaving Kolbe Corp, 199–202
    mentoring relationship with Amy, 124–27
    pre-FOB contract, 77–78
    values shared with FMs, 25–27
Kolbe A Index
    overview, 44–47, **232**
    as analysis vs. guessing, 135
    and MO, 15–17
    Range of Success, FM compared to ideal candidate, 113
    and role assignments, 60, 113
    statistics from, 48
    Synergy Analysis, 161
    test-retest reliability research, 223
Kolbe Bottom Lines booklet, 234
Kolbe Certification, 232
Kolbe Coaching Reports, 233
Kolbe Corp
    overview, 7–8
    fire destroys office, 184–85
    Kathy questions Amy's pizza order for staff meeting, 195–96
    research, 221–24
    Takes Two program, 80
    theft of intellectual property, 67
    transition from Kathy as CEO to David and Amy in charge, 199–202
Kolbe Creative Process, **227**
Kolbe Indexes, 143, 232–33. *See also* Kolbe A Index
Kolbe Leadership Analytics, 157–58
Kolbe Leadership Training, 231
Kolbe RightFit Hiring System, 134–35, 235
Kolbe Strengths, **227**
Kolbe TeamSuccess Seminar for Family Businesses, 231
Kolbe Theory of Conation, 227–28
    Action Modes, 208–09

axioms relating to individual
    actions or MOs, 211–14
axioms relating to interactions or
    group behaviors, 216–17
axioms relating to interactions or
    relationships, 214–16
mental factors/parts of the mind,
    207–08
use of time and energy, 217–18
Zones of Operation in the Action
    Modes, 209–11
Kolbe Y(outh) Index, 143

L

leadership
    and betrayals, 66–67
    level of effort in FOBs, 40
    sharing stories of backstage goofs,
        127
    of teams, 159–60
    and transitions, 173–75, 193–95
    trusting their own instincts,
        53–55, 57
    values of leaders, 21–22, 28–29
    See also role placement of FMs
Leadership Analytics, 157–58,
    234–35
Leadership Training, 231
levels of effort, **226**

M

marriage partners. *See* couples
matrix organizations, 168
meetings vs. personal conversations,
    103
mental energy, **228**
mental energy management, 41–43
mental factors. *See* affect/affective part
    of the mind; cognition/cognitive
    part of the mind; conation/cona-
    tive part of the mind
mental muscle development, 140. *See*

also next-generation ambition
    development
mentoring relationship development,
    124–27
mistakes, learning from, 127
mistakes vs. unethical behavior, 69
modus operandi (MO)
    overview, 13, **228**
    and Action Modes, 43–44
    and children, 148
    examples, 15–16
    of family members, 59–60
    gender bias and birth order myths,
        132–33
    instincts as conative MO, 54–55
    listening to your own gut first, 57
    mentors and, 124–27
    and risk taking, 79
    and role placement of FMs,
        112–14
    and spouses working together,
        78–81
    of team members, 160–65

N

next-generation ambition develop-
    ment, 139–54
    overview, 139
    confidence vs. arrogance, 144–46
    decision making skill development,
        146–47
    empowerment, 140
    helping kids play to their strengths,
        147–48
    listening to your children, 148–49
    and professional growth opportu-
        nities in FOBs, 149–51
    providing real, useful work,
        152–53
    providing variety for internship at
        FOB, 152
    sowing seeds of success, 140–44

next-generation changes and values, 182

non–family members (NFMs)
  barriers between FMs and, 87–89
  betrayal by FOB, 65, 66
  betrayal by NFM, 66–67
  as FM "babysitters," 130–32
  and FM efforts to rebuild trust, 71
  FM integration with, 27–28
  and FM lingo, 93, 101, 107
  hiring considerations, 37–38
  opportunities to earn trust, 63–65
  transparency and honesty with, 103–04
  and work ethic of FMs, 23–24
nonprofit organizations, 40–41
nonverbal communication, 99–100

O

open space for teams, 165–66
organization development, 5, 7–8
outside advisors as facilitators, 89–90

P

parents
  allowing hard work, 139
  denial example, 23–24
  and child's manager, 126–27
  and payback for child's education, 114–15
  teaching choice-making skills, 146–47
  trusting their child, 58–59
  and untrustworthy children, 61–63
penalties and reparation for betray-als, 70
performance evaluations, 167–70
perseverance and resilience, 140. See also next-generation ambition development

personal brand by Action Mode, 43–50
  overview, 43–44
  accommodating action, 48
  Initiating Action, 44–46
  maximizing conative strengths, 48–50
  resisting action, 46–47
phone calls for communicating, 102–03
placement of FMs. See role placement of FMs
policy transitions, 179–80
presentations with other FMs, 100–02
prevent. See CounterAct
problem solving
  creative problem solving, 139, 142, 148–49
  and instincts, 54, 57
professional firms and FMs, 11–12
professional growth opportunities in FOBs, 149–51

Q

Quick Start behavior
  overview, 14, 15–16, **228**
  and drive to initiate risk, 78–79
  as innovators, 45
  as Stabilizers, 47
Quick Start CounterActors, 79, 94, 177–78
Quick Start Initiators, 45, 79, 81, 94, 151, 163, 178, 194, 200

R

Range of Success, 113
Rapp, Will, 7–8, 77–78, 98
ReAct/ReActions (accommodating), 17–18, 48, **228**
realistic expectations, 121–22
Reality Checks

overview, 5

boundaries, 90

communication, 107

level of effort, 52

graceful exits, 203

identifying innate strengths, 17,
    18–19

next-generation ambition develop-
    ment, 153–54

teams, 171

transition orchestration, 191

trust, 71

values, 33

recognition of work well done,
    167–70

reparation and penalties for betrayals,
    70–71

research, 221–24

researchers. See *entries beginning with*
    Fact Finder

resentment of offspring toward FOB,
    119–20

return on investment (ROI) issues,
    136

RightFit Hiring System, 134–35, 235

risks and risk taking, 78–79, 156

role placement of FMs

    guesses based on family knowl-
        edge, 59–61

    guidelines, 111–12

    and measures of productivity,
        188–89

    next-generation interns, 152

    value-added requirement, 8–9,
        23–25, 123–24

    See also FM development

S

sibling rivalries, 81–84

siblings playing and working together,
    156

Simplifier Fact Finder, 46

social conditioning, conative research
    on, 133

social media, 101–02

strain, **228**

Striving Instinct, **228**

success, principles for, 4–5

sustainable success, 7–19

    building on FMs strengths, 9–14

    FM/FOB conative mismatch
        example, 9–12, 15–18

    and FM/NFM integration, 27–28

    FM's value-added requirement,
        8–9, 23–25

    and founder's values, 21–22

    Kolbe Corp example, 7–8

Synergy, 135, 160–65, 162, **228**

T

Takes Two, 80, 235

teams, 155–71

    overview, 155–56

    collaborative, 9, 157, 165

    hybrid teams, 100–01, 157–160,
        165, 168

    independent work by team mem-
        bers, 156–158, 166–67

    interdependent teams, 9, 156–57,
        165

    leadership based on structure,
        159–60

    morale issues at multilevel market-
        ing company, 169–70

    recognizing individual and interac-
        tive contributions, 167–69

    space considerations, 165–66

    Synergistic team, 162

    Synergy and MOs of team mem-
        bers, 160–65

TeamSuccess Seminar for Family Busi-
    nesses, 231

tension, **229**

thinking vs. instincts, 53–54. *See also*

conation/conative part of the mind

tornado destroys an FOB, 183

transition orchestration, 173–91

overview, 173–77

conative strengths and outlook on transitions, 177–81

decision making process, 173–75

founder leaving, 196–97, 199–202

involving key influencers, 181–82

and job security, 186–87

planning for worst-case scenarios, 183–85

policy transitions, 179–80

power struggles as impetus, 185–86

terminating an FM, 187–90

turning over a business, 175–77

trust, 53–71

overview, 53

of behavior in crises, 61–63

blind trust, 23–24, 55, 59

breaking trust, 65–69

developing with actions, 106–07

false or unrealistic expectations as basis for, 59–61

and FMs' instinct-based truths, 58–59

gut check, 55–57

NFMs opportunities to earn trust, 63–65

protection from mistakes vs., 127–29

repairing broken trust, 69–71

and transparent, honest, realistic communication, 103–04

trusting your instincts, 51, 53–55, 220–21

U

ugly exit prevention, 197–99

V

value-added requirement for FMs, 8–9, 23–25, 123–24

values, 21–33

overview, 21–22

applying, 25–27

assessing, 27–28

breach of trust, 63

communicating with actions, 106–07

competing values, 31–33

importance of, 22–25

inappropriate imposition of, 29–31

integration into work environment, 107

next-generation changes, 182

practicing, 28–29, 122

and transitions, 176–77

and transparent, honest, realistic communication, 103–04

W

worst-case scenario planning for transitions, 183–85

Z

Zones of Operation in Action Modes, 15–18, 209–11. *See also* personal brand by Action Mode